my fussy eater

my fussy eater

CIARA ATTWELL

A REAL MUM'S EASY
EVERYDAY RECIPES
FOR THE WHOLE FAMILY

This book is dedicated to Aoife and Fintan

Published by Lagom
An imprint of Bonnier Publishing
The Plaza,
535 Kings Road,
Chelsea Harbour,
London SW10 0SZ

www.bonnierpublishing.com

Hardback ISBN: 978 1 911 60075 6
eBook ISBN: 978 1 911 60076 3

A CIP catalogue of this book is available from the British Library.

Cover design by Emily Rough
Content designed by Mark Golden at Crazy Monkey Creative
Food styling by Rebecca Woods
Printed and bound by Gráficas Estella

1 3 5 7 9 10 8 6 4 2

CONTENTS

INTRODUCTION 6

    WHO IS THIS BOOK FOR? 8

    MY FOOD PHILOSOPHY 8

    LET'S TALK ABOUT SUGAR 9

    TIPS FOR FUSSY EATING 10

    HOW TO USE THIS BOOK 14

    KITCHEN ESSENTIALS 15

    MEAL PLANS 17

BREAKFAST 20

    MAKE AHEAD 22

    WEEKEND 34

LUNCH 46

    QUICK AND EASY 48

    FREEZER FRIENDLY 60

    LUNCHBOX IDEAS 68

FAMILY MEALS 72

    PASTA, RICE AND NOODLES 74

    MEAT 90

    FISH 104

    BURGERS 110

    VEGGIE SIDES 116

SNACKS 124

    BATCH-MADE 126

    FROZEN TREATS 138

    BREAD AND CRACKERS 146

SWEET THINGS AND DRINKS 154

    DESSERTS AND CAKES 156

    DRINKS 166

DIPS AND SAUCES 176

    SWEET 178

    SAVOURY 184

INDEX 188

ACKNOWLEDGEMENTS 192

INTRODUCTION

Hello. I'm Ciara, mum to seven-year-old Aoife and four-year-old Fintan. Originally from Ireland, I now live in the UK with my husband and children where I run the website My Fussy Eater. Since starting my blog in 2014 I have had an overwhelming response to my recipes and my tips and tricks for making feeding kids a little easier. There is nothing more heartwarming than to receive messages from other mums and dads telling me how their kids have gobbled up one of my dishes. I'm now really excited to be able to share more than 100 tasty food ideas to get not only your fussy eaters, but the whole family, eating a wider range of delicious and nutritious meals and snacks.

Most people are surprised when I tell them that I am not a natural cook. I spent my student years living off pasta and jars of tomato sauce with the odd bit of minced beef or chicken thrown in if I was feeling flush that week. Working long hours in London in my twenties meant I ate out a lot or relied on supermarket ready-meals. Even when my daughter was born in 2011 I never really embraced home cooking. I went back to work when she was six months old and she was weaned by our fantastic childminder at the time, who had her eating everything including curries, stews and all kinds of vegetables by the time she was eight months old.

The shock came when I left my job and we moved out of London a year later. Aoife went from eating breakfast, lunch and dinner at the childminder's, to me preparing all her meals and snacks. I took for granted all the hard work that our childminder had done with weaning and introducing Aoife to a wide variety of different foods. She gradually became more and more fussy, not helped by the fact that I was then pregnant with our second child and living pretty much solely on a diet of beige food!

When Fintan was born in January 2014 my appetite for normal food came back and I set about trying to improve the whole family's eating habits. I started www.myfussyeater.com and began sharing the recipes I was making, along with little tips and tricks that were working for us to improve Aoife's picky eating. Slowly her diet improved and she began eating a wider variety of foods. Now, at the age of seven, we still struggle to get her to eat certain foods or to try new things. As lovely as it would be, there's no quick-fix cure for fussy eating. The subject of food and feeding is something we have to focus on as parents from weaning right up to their teenage years, but at the same time it shouldn't dominate family life and cause unnecessary stress every day. That's why I try to make all my recipes as quick and easy as possible, using simple ingredients that you can buy in any supermarket. Minimal stress, maximum taste and a happy family!

WHO IS THIS BOOK FOR?

This is a cookbook created with fussy eaters in mind but with food that the whole family will enjoy. The recipes are designed to expand your family's diet and get everyone eating a little healthier and with a lot more fresh produce. There will be some recipes that your kids will love and others that they'll hate – that's inevitable! – but it's the small changes that you make that will have the greatest impact over time. Start experimenting with new foods and flavours and your fussy eater may just surprise you. Above all, have fun and enjoy the food you eat together as a family.

MY FOOD PHILOSOPHY

Nowadays most parents are well aware of the importance of a good diet and proper nutrition for their children. Rather than having a lack of information in this area, many parents I speak to feel bombarded with advice from all different angles, much of it often conflicting. Which approach to weaning is best, baby-led or purée? How much sugar is too much? Are carbs good or bad? Is it 5 or 10 portions of fruit and vegetables a child should eat a day?

Having lots of differing opinions and information at our fingertips can be a really powerful tool when it comes to parenting but sometimes it can also hinder us. Feeding our children shouldn't be confusing, complicated or ridden with guilt, nor should we feel like we need a qualification in childhood nutrition to make a simple evening meal. For this reason my family food philosophy is simple:

Balance – I strive to find a balance between serving up proper nutritious food and meals that my family will actually eat.

Fruit and veg – I pack as much fruit and vegetables into my meals and snacks as possible, some 'hidden' and some eaten whole.

Water – I encourage my children to drink mostly water (and lots of it), with squash and juice being a treat a couple of times a week.

At times when I feel overwhelmed at home or when I am dealing with a particularly picky phase with one of my children, I find that concentrating on these three simple goals makes the job of feeding my family a lot less stressful and far more manageable. I would encourage you to pick a few simple food goals or philosophies that matter to you, and keep them at the forefront of your mind whenever you are struggling with food and feeding issues at home.

LET'S TALK ABOUT SUGAR

I don't think it's possible to talk about family food without mentioning sugar. Extensive research has proven the link between overconsumption of sugar and childhood obesity. With fast food, processed meals and sugary drinks and snacks being more accessible to our children now than ever before, it is important for us as parents to limit these kinds of foods and model healthy eating for them. But again, the idea of balance is key for me. Yes, my children eat sugar. Aoife loves nothing more than a massive slice of carrot cake and Finn's treat of choice will always be an indulgent chocolate brownie. But these foods are treats, to be enjoyed a few times a week and not several times a day.

Day to day I try to limit sugar in our family's diet, but I don't completely cut it out. You will notice that I do use sugar in some of my recipes – mainly cookies and cakes – as it is very difficult to replicate the texture and taste of sugar in these foods without using an artificial alternative. Instead, I try to use less sugar than you may typically find in the shop-bought versions.

With other sweet snacks and desserts I use the natural sweetness of fruit and also honey or maple syrup. Sugar is still sugar in any form – white sugar, fruit sugar, coconut sugar, honey, maple syrup - all will have the same effect on the body if consumed in excess.

However, refined sugar is higher on the glycemic index than honey, meaning it will raise blood sugar levels quicker. Also, honey is a more concentrated source of sweetness than sugar so I use less of it in my cooking.

I would encourage you to do your own research and use your own discretion when deciding how to sweeten your child's food: you can swap honey for maple syrup, sugar or any other sweeteners in my recipes.

TIPS FOR FUSSY EATING

For a lot of parents a big cause of stress and arguments at home is food and fussy eating. Food plays such a major part in all our lives. Aside from its functional role to provide energy and keep us alive, food is so important within family units and a wider social circle. We have an innate instinct to feed and nourish. We use food to celebrate, to comfort and to console. So, when our children refuse to eat it can cause a huge amount of guilt, stress and tension.

My tips for dealing with fussy eating come from my own experience with two picky children, but I know that every family is different. Use these tips as a guide as to how you can approach fussy eating in your house but remember that this list is by no way exhaustive or prescriptive. Experiment and find out what works for you. No two children are the same and you may even find that you will need to have a different approach for every child.

It's also important to point out that these tips are aimed at parents of moderate fussy eaters. If you have a child who is an extremely picky eater and are worried about their weight or nutritional intake then seek advice from your doctor, paediatrician or health care worker.

1. RELAX

The first piece of advice I always give to parents when asked about fussy eating is to relax and try not to let the situation get too stressful. Most parents admit that they deal with fussy eating at some point in their child's life so you are not alone. Picky eating can strike at any stage – during weaning, with a toddler or even an older child all the way up to late teens. So please try not to get too stressed about it and above all don't blame yourself.

Parenting these days seems to come with a lot of guilt and blame but the fact that you are concerned about your child's eating and motivated to improve it already means that you are doing a fantastic job!

2. UNDERSTAND WHY IT'S HAPPENING

Half the battle in tackling fussy eating is to understand why it's happening to begin with. A lot of parents breeze through weaning and then struggle to understand how a baby who ate everything can suddenly turn into an extremely picky toddler who refuses almost everything put in front of him.

It is very common for toddlers to start exerting their newly found independence through food. From the age of two, toddlers realise that they have control over certain elements of their lives – the toys they play with, the programmes they watch on TV, the clothes they wear and, unfortunately, the food that they eat. So while it might be confusing for parents to understand how their veggie-loving baby has suddenly turned into a very fussy toddler, be assured that it is a very normal consequence of their budding sense of independence and control.

Similarly, when older children start school and begin to pay more attention to what their friends are doing, it can be very common for them to start questioning the food they eat at home. Peer pressure, whether direct or indirect, can massively influence a child's outlook on food. Again, this is a very normal part of a child growing up and becoming influenced by people and situations outside of their immediate family.

By understanding the root cause of fussy eating, it makes it a lot easier for us as parents to try to overcome it.

3. SLOW INTRODUCTIONS

It is really important to remember that most children do not have the same excitement or anticipation around new foods that adults do; in fact, quite the opposite. Most children are at best wary and at worst downright suspicious of any kind of food that's remotely out of the ordinary for them.

Most children need to be offered a new food 10 to 15 times before they will accept it and eventually eat it. I know this may seem like a very slow method to get them to eat new things but you can start by introducing foods in really easy ways. So, if for example you really want your child to eat some broccoli, firstly have it on the dinner table regularly. Let them see it and let them see you eating it. Next, encourage them to try just a very small amount, making it clear that if they don't like it then they don't have to have any more. A few days later you could try introducing it again but in a different format – try adding very small amounts to a pasta sauce or mash it up and mix it with other vegetables that they like. Slowly over time you may be able to get them to eat a little bit more, so do keep on persevering!

4. ONE STEP AT A TIME

It can be tempting for us as adults to want to go all out with our plans to improve our family's diet, announcing a complete overhaul, throwing out all 'junk' food and filling the kitchen with myriad new foods, fruits and veggies. But it's crucial where children are concerned to take small steps and make gentle changes.

Introduce new foods one at a time. It's important to keep an element of familiarity with a child's food. So, for example, you might want to encourage them to swap white bread toast at breakfast every morning for something more nutritious. Don't just present them with an entirely new breakfast. Change one little element every few days: instead of two slices of white toast, give them one slice and one slice of Porridge Bread (see page 29). A couple of days later add a few strawberries or slices of apple to the side. Slowly over the course of a couple of weeks you may be able to leave the toast out completely. Your child will respond a lot better to these slow changes rather than a complete overhaul of their meals.

5. POSITIVE LANGUAGE

The way we talk about food and eating is hugely important to all children and not just fussy eaters. I try as much as possible to always talk about food in a positive way. When my daughter doesn't want to eat her vegetables I explain what the nutrients in those veggies will do for her – to help her hair grow, to make her bones strong. Similarly, when I am trying to get her to eat something wholegrain and filling like oats for breakfast, rather than white bread, I explain how the oats will keep her full and provide enough energy for her to learn and play at school.

Focusing on the positive rather than the negative helps to set children up for a good lifelong relationship with food, moving away from the 'good vs bad' outlook on food and instead striving for a balanced attitude.

6. GET THEM INVOLVED

Getting my kids into the kitchen has been instrumental in getting them to eat a more varied diet. We know that kids love baking cookies and cakes but when it comes to picky eating, it's important for them to be involved in the day-to-day food preparation and cooking that happens at home. For toddlers it can be as simple as taking them to the fridge or store cupboard and allowing them to choose which vegetables you cook for dinner. Or let them stand on a chair by the work surface and help you to make a sandwich for lunch.

When you are in a rush to prepare meals at home I know that it's not always possible to let them help. On days like this I let my son play with a few ingredients instead – I give him some soft veggies and a plastic knife to cut them or a bowl with some flour and water to mix together. He thinks he's helping me cook while I actually get on with making dinner!

The older your child is, the more responsibility you can give them in the kitchen but any kind of involvement is bound to make them more interested in their food when it actually reaches the table. Drawing up meal plans with older children works really well too (see page 17). I sometimes struggle to get my daughter to eat something nutritious and filling for breakfast, so last year we started writing up a Breakfast Meal Plan for the week. She chooses whatever she likes to eat on a Saturday and Sunday (it's usually a hot cross bun one day and a bacon sandwich the next!). We then decide together on five more nutritious breakfasts to have during the week. This system works really well and she enjoys ticking off each day once she's cleared her plate.

7. MAKE IT FUN

Mealtimes can be a little dull for children so try injecting a bit of fun into them and introduce as much colour as you can in both the food and the crockery. Experiment with lots of different plates.

You can pick them up really cheaply online or in pound shops. My kids love compartment plates: they are a lot more fun than plain white plates and they're fantastic for fussy eaters who don't like the different food elements of their meals to be touching.

Snack plates are also fantastic as they can encourage children to eat a variety of fruit and veg along with a small sweet treat. I post a lot of images of snack plates on my social media and I always get sent so many questions about them. Again, you don't have to spend a lot of money: keep an eye out in your local pound shop.

8. BREAK THE ROUTINE

Most advice you read about fussy eating and feeding children recommends eating together at the table as much as possible. While sitting down together as a family to eat is hugely beneficial in so many ways, it can also be just as helpful to change up your usual feeding routine, especially if it's not working for your fussy eater.

If your child associates sitting down to a family meal with stress, then removing them from this situation is the most immediate change you can make. Carpet or garden picnics are also a great way to move a picky eating child away from the anxiety of the dinner table. Give them a little bit of space and the freedom to take their time eating without expectant eyes on them.

People are often surprised that I frequently let my children roam around the house during mealtimes. I know this method will not suit every family but it really works for us. My kids will often have a few bites of food, leave the table to play and return a little later for some more. It may take them 30 or 40 minutes to finish their food but the important thing to me is that they are eating and it's stress free. Experiment with different ways to break mealtime routines in your house and you may be surprised how well your child responds.

9. HIDDEN VEGGIES

This topic can sometimes be a little controversial! I know that not all parents agree with hiding vegetable from children and instead believe it's better to encourage children to eat them in their whole form. I completely understand this but I also know what it's like to deal with picky eaters who will refuse point blank to eat most veggies. So, if you have to resort to hiding them, don't feel bad!

I feed my children a combination of hidden veggie meals and vegetables in their whole form and this method is working well for us. The recipes in this book feature a mixture of both hidden and whole veg so pick and choose which suit you and your child best.

10. SENSORY ISSUES

For many children, their difficulties with food are actually sensory based. My son is autistic and over the past year I have become increasingly aware that his issues with food go deeper than just being a picky child. ASD children are commonly more hyper- or hypo-sensitive to food and how it looks, tastes, smells and feels. This will have a very big impact on the types of food that they want to eat and can make the whole issue of feeding and mealtimes even more challenging than normal.

Many neuro-typical children will experience similar sensory reactions to food so it is worth bearing this mind if you have a particularly fussy child. Using the strategies I have outlined above has helped improve my son's eating but it is still something we have to work on every day.

HOW TO USE THIS BOOK

I deliberated how I should group the recipes in this book for some time. In the end I settled on a traditional breakdown of Breakfast – Lunch – Family Meals – Snacks, etc., as it is the format that most of us are familiar with. I have also broken those sections down further, for example breakfasts that can be made ahead for a busy week or as something to cook on a more leisurely weekend. I really would encourage you to just treat these headings as a guide only and to pick and choose recipes based on how you and your family eat.

MIX IT UP!

Many children, including mine, eat better earlier in the day. I try to make breakfast and lunch as nutritious and filling as possible. By 5p.m. they are usually tired, with little energy and motivation to tuck into a big evening meal and start trying new foods. Make the Family Meal recipes for lunchtime, try the Breakfast recipes for teatime, play around until you find a mealtime rhythm that suits you and your family. And if you end up serving dinner leftovers for breakfast, then that's completely okay!

INFO ICONS

Included in each recipe are icons that show:

GF	Gluten-free recipes or where you can make easy substitutions that can make it gluten free
DF	Dairy-free recipes or where you can make easy substitutions that can make it dairy free
FR	Freezer-friendly recipes
BC	Batch-cook recipes
KM	Recipes that kids can help to make

PORTION SIZES

Portion sizes will of course depend on the age of your children and their appetite. Use the serving sizes as a guide and decrease or increase the serving as you see fit. Where a recipe serves four, this is based on an average family of two adults and two children.

SEASONING

Use your discretion when it comes to seasoning these recipes with salt and pepper. Additional salt and pepper seasoning is optional in all the recipes. I generally use reduced sodium soy sauce and stock cubes in all my recipes.

RED WINE

I use a small amount of red wine in a few recipes in this book. When the wine is cooked at a high temperature the majority of the alcohol content will be evaporated and so it is safe for children. If, however, you would prefer not to use wine, then it can be easily replaced with the same quantity of stock.

KITCHEN ESSENTIALS

For me, being prepared and having a well-stocked kitchen is vital when trying to get to grips with feeding my family three times a day. Below are all the gadgets I use to make meal and snack prep that little bit easier, along with the ingredients that I always have on hand. But please don't rush out and buy everything I have listed here: just pick and choose the gadgets and ingredients that you will use the most depending on the recipes your family enjoys.

And when it comes to store cupboard goods in particular, like nuts, seeds, quinoa and oils, try to buy these in bulk. They will last a long time in your cupboard, in sealed jars or containers, and work out much cheaper in the end. The same goes for frozen fruit and vegetables – don't presume that fresh is always best. Frozen produce is often cheaper, still nutritious and of course lasts longer, meaning you waste less.

MY FAVOURITE KITCHEN GADGETS

Food processor – this doesn't have to be expensive. Whatever your budget you should be able to get a good food processor. I use mine several times a week so it's definitely money well spent.

Stand blender – again, you don't have to buy a pricey blender, but they are brilliant for smoothies and blitzing pasta sauces.

Hand-held blender – a cheaper option ideal for soups and my homemade mayo (see page 185).

Electric whisk – to beat eggs, whip cream, etc. Big stand mixers are lovely but they are not essential for any of my recipes.

Electric scales – you can pick these up really cheaply online. They are much easier to use and of course more accurate than old-style weighing scales and take up far less room, too.

Garlic crusher – this takes all the faff out of chopping garlic.

Ice cream scoop – this is one of my favourite kitchen hacks. I use an ice cream scoop to transfer muffin batter to muffin cases; this honestly is easier than using a spoon!

Silicone baking sheet – this is a great alternative to baking parchment and can be used whenever I mention in a recipe to line a baking tray or baking sheet. They are re-useable and really easy to wash.

Silicone muffin cases – not only are these re-usable but they are non-stick, too. They work much better than paper cases when making healthier muffins and cupcakes and can also be used to serve up snacks to the kids, too.

Colourful plates, bowls and cutlery – I talk more about this in my Tips for Fussy Eating (see page 10) but for me an array of colourful and fun plates just for the kids is essential.

Good lunchboxes – you don't have to spend a fortune on lunchboxes but it is worth shopping around to make sure you are buying something that is easy to clean, is shatterproof and has enough space for a decent-sized lunch for your child.

STORE CUPBOARD ESSENTIALS
Dried goods
Pasta
Rice
Noodles
Rolled oats
Quinoa
Flour (plain, wholemeal and self-raising)
Cornflour
Baking powder
Bicarbonate of soda (or baking soda)
Nuts
Seeds
Flaxseed
Chia seeds
Cocoa powder (unsweetened)
Stock cubes (low salt)

Tins, jars, cartons and bottles
Tinned tomatoes
Tomato purée
Passata
Tinned chickpeas
Tinned cannellini beans
Lentils (dried and tinned)
Tuna
Coconut milk
Honey
Vanilla extract
Soy sauce (reduced sodium)
Olive oil
Coconut oil
Peanut butter

Herbs and spices
Dried Italian or mixed herbs
Dried oregano
Paprika (smoked and plain)
Mild curry powder
Mild chilli powder
Ground cumin
Ground cinnamon
Garlic powder

FRESH AND FROZEN ESSENTIALS
Fruit and vegetables
Bananas
Apples
Pears
Seasonal berries
Onions
Garlic
Potatoes
Sweet potato
Carrots
Courgette
Peppers
Cucumber
Spring onions

Dairy, meat and eggs
Unsalted butter
Greek yoghurt
Cheddar cheese
Cooked chicken or ham
Dairy or non-dairy milk
Eggs (all eggs are medium free-range
    unless otherwise specified)

Frozen goods
Chopped mixed veggies
Peas
Sweetcorn
Puff pastry
Breadcrumbs (blitz stale bread in the food
    processor to make breadcrumbs then store
    in freezer bags)
Berries and tropical fruit

MEAL PLANS

Don't underestimate the benefits of meal planning when it comes to improving your family's eating habits. Planning ahead will help to ensure you are adding lots of variety to your children's diet over the course of the week as well as lots of other benefits, including:

Less food waste – as you are maximising ingredients and using up leftovers

Saving money – as you are planning ahead and buying ingredients in bulk and in the cheapest shops, rather than relying on more expensive smaller stores or even takeaways

Less stress – as you no longer have that 5p.m. panic of what to make for dinner

Saving time – as you can batch-cook popular meals and pop half in the freezer for another day

I have set out four weeks of meal plans based around the recipes in this book. I have tried to plan a variety of different meals and nutrients throughout the week while also maximising ingredients and minimising the time spent cooking. Batch-cooking and using your freezer will help to save so much time. If you know next week is going to be hectic, batch-cook and freeze some meals this week to make those busy days a little easier.

These meal plans are of course just a guide. Feel free to chop and change them depending on what recipes you like. To get started, try meal planning just a couple of days a week. I promise you won't regret it. Meal planning is also a great way to get the kids more involved in their food. Give them a few different options and allow them to plan some of the meals. It will give them a sense of control over what they are eating and encourage them to take more of an interest in your family's food.

MEAL PLAN: WEEK 1

	BREAKFAST	LUNCH	DINNER	SNACK/PUDDING
MONDAY	Chocolate Banana Overnight Oats See page 28	Tomato and Lentil Soup See page 56	Batch-cook Bolognese See page 79	Peanut Butter Brownies See page 161
TUESDAY	Porridge Bread See page 29	Hidden Veggie Sausage Rolls See page 62	Lentil Veggie Burger See page 111	Mango, Lime and Coconut Energy Bites See page 128
WEDNESDAY	Chocolate Granola See page 23	Cheese and Chive Rolls See page 61	Sweet and Sour Chicken See page 95	Chocolate Nut Frozen Yoghurt Bark See page 141
THURSDAY	Egg and Spinach Breakfast Pockets See page 36	Spinach and Cheese Muffins See page 67	Pesto Salmon Bake with Couscous See page 106	Oaty Chocolate Biscuits See page 134
FRIDAY	Strawberry Quinoa Breakfast Bars See page 24	Tuna Bites See page 55	Hidden Veggie Tomato Sauce with Pasta See page 82	Fruit Salad Popsicle See page 143
SATURDAY	Veggie Egg Scramble See page 35	Broccoli and Cheese Quesadilla See page 53	Tropical Chicken Burger See page 112	Chocolate Chip Peanut Butter Muffins See page 136
SUNDAY	Healthier Pop Tarts See page 42	Veggie Pizza Roll-ups See page 65	Beef and Pearl Barley Casserole See page 99	Raspberry Chia Crumble Squares See page 163

MEAL PLAN: WEEK 2

	BREAKFAST	LUNCH	DINNER	SNACK/PUDDING
MONDAY	Beans on Toast See page 39	Cheesy Chicken Fritters See page 59	Cheese and Tomato Baked Risotto See page 87	Watermelon and Kiwi Popsicle See page 142
TUESDAY	Fruit and Nut Breakfast Cookies See page 27	Toastie Pitta Pockets See page 54	Chicken and Aubergine Katsu See page 94	Carrot and Orange Greek Yoghurt Muffins See page 135
WEDNESDAY	Strawberry Shortcake Overnight Oats See page 28	Tortilla Quiche See page 50	One-pot Salmon Linguine See page 109	Raspberry Ripple Nice-cream See page 145
THURSDAY	Strawberry Banana Bread See page 33	Chicken and Veggie Frittata Fingers See page 49	Chicken, Chorizo and Prawn Paella See page 84	Fruity Flapjacks See page 127
FRIDAY	Fruity Pancakes See page 41	Cauliflower Cheese Cakes See page 66	Loaded Nachos See page 100	Chocolate Chip Energy Bites See page 128
SATURDAY	Sweet Potato Hash Browns See page 35	Hidden Veggie Sausage Rolls See page 62	Seven Veg Lentil Lasagne See page 83	Rhubarb and Strawberry Custard Pots See page 160
SUNDAY	Caramelised Banana Breakfast Parfait See page 45	Spinach and Cheese Muffins See page 67	Piri Piri Spatchcock Chicken See page 92	Chocolate Orange Tart See page 158

MEAL PLAN: WEEK 3

	BREAKFAST	LUNCH	DINNER	SNACK/PUDDING
MONDAY	Banana and Blueberry Loaves See page 30	Toastie Pitta Pockets See page 54	Tuna Meatballs See page 105	Yoghurt Pudding Pops See page 139
TUESDAY	Chocolate Granola See page 23	Cheesy Chicken Fritters See page 59	Fruity Veggie Curry See page 89	Raspberry Chia Jam Pastry Straws See page 148
WEDNESDAY	Strawberry Banana Bread See page 33	Tomato and Lentil Soup See page 56	Toad in the Hole See page 103	Strawberry and Chocolate Popsicle See page 143
THURSDAY	Breakfast Frittata See page 38	Chicken and Veggie Frittata Fingers See page 49	Popeye's Protein Pesto with Pasta See page 78	Fruity Flapjacks See page 127
FRIDAY	Porridge Bread See page 29	Cheese and Chive Rolls See page 61	Smoky Meatball Pasta Bake See page 81	Raspberry Coconut Energy Bites See page 130
SATURDAY	Strawberry Quinoa Breakfast Bars See page 24	Broccoli and Cheese Quesadilla See page 53	Sesame Chicken Noodles See page 76	Healthier Eton Mess See page 157
SUNDAY	Camaralised Banana Breakfast Parfait See page 45	Cauliflower Cheese Cakes See page 66	Greek Chicken Traybake See page 97	Finn's Sweet Potato Chocolate Cake See page 164

MEAL PLAN: WEEK 4

	BREAKFAST	LUNCH	DINNER	SNACK/PUDDING
MONDAY	Veggie Egg Scramble See page 35	Tortilla Quiche See page 50	Melty Mozzarella Beef Burger See page 115	Chocolate Orange Energy Bites See page 130
TUESDAY	Sweet Potato Hash Browns See page 35	Tuna Bites See page 55	Chicken Dippers with Honey Mustard Mayo See page 98	Pesto Pastry Straws See page 148
WEDNESDAY	Chocolate Banana Overnight Oats See page 28	Hidden Veggie Sausage Rolls See page 62	Creamy Roasted Pepper Sauce with Pasta See page 75	Mint Choc Chip Nice-cream See page 145
THURSDAY	Banana and Blueberry Loaves See page 30	Spinach and Cheese Muffins See page 67	Sweet and Sour Chicken See page 95	Chocolate Chip Granola Bars See page 131
FRIDAY	Fruit and Nut Breakfast Cookies See page 27	Toastie Pitta Pockets See page 54	Apple and Carrot Chicken Balls See page 91	Mango and Coconut Popsicle See page 142
SATURDAY	Beans on Toast See page 39	Cheesy Chicken Fritters See page 59	Hidden Veggie Risotto See page 86	Aoife's Carrot Cake See page 165
SUNDAY	Egg and Spinach Breakfast Pockets See page 36	Veggie Pizza Roll-ups See page 65	Pesto Salmon Bake with Couscous See page 106	No-sugar Rice Pudding See page 157

BREAKFAST

MAKE AHEAD

We all know that breakfast is the most important meal of the day but it also tends to be the busiest time in most households. With so much to do before we get the kids out of the door to school every morning, it can be all too easy to turn to processed sugary cereals. But it is so important that we fuel little bodies and brains with good, wholesome food for a busy day ahead.

All of these breakfast recipes can be made in advance and will keep for several days in a container in the fridge or cupboard, making them perfect for getting a head start on the week!

CHOCOLATE GRANOLA

| Serves: 15 | Prep time: 5 minutes | Cook time: 30 minutes |

This homemade granola is much cheaper and healthier than the shop-bought stuff, which is often loaded with sugar. You can flavour it to your own tastes – my kids love this chocolate version! It fills a really big jar, keeps for a couple of weeks and is perfect with milk, added to yoghurt or sprinkled over a smoothie.

Ingredients

120g mixed nuts (I use cashews, walnuts, pecans and almonds)

220g rolled oats

50g desiccated coconut

20g mixed seeds (I use pumpkin and sunflower seeds)

2 tbsp cocoa powder

2 tbsp coconut oil

4 tbsp honey

½ tsp vanilla extract

60g dried fruit (I use raisins, chopped apricots and cranberries)

Method

1. Preheat the oven to 160°C/140°C Fan/Gas Mark 3 and line 2 large baking trays with baking parchment.

2. Chop or break the nuts into smaller pieces if making granola for small children. Mix the nuts in a bowl with the oats, desiccated coconut, seeds and cocoa powder.

3. Melt the coconut oil in the microwave or in a small saucepan on the hob, then add to the bowl, along with the honey and vanilla extract. Mix well until all the ingredients are well coated.

4. Divide the mixture between the lined trays and bake in the oven for 30 minutes, stirring the granola twice during that time, until dark brown (but not burnt).

5. Remove the trays from the oven and mix in the dried fruit. Leave to cool before serving.

6. Store in an airtight jar for up to 2 weeks.

STRAWBERRY QUINOA BREAKFAST BARS

| Makes: 9 bars | Prep time: 5 minutes | Cook time: 20–25 minutes |

A tasty and filling breakfast bar, crammed full of healthy ingredients.
These nutritious bars are perfect for the whole family
and are a great grab-and-go breakfast.

Ingredients

2 medium ripe bananas

2 eggs

½ tsp vanilla extract

100g cooked quinoa (30g uncooked)

150g rolled oats

30g raisins

100g strawberries, hulled and
   roughly chopped

Method

1. Preheat the oven to 200°C/180°C Fan/Gas Mark 6
   and line a 20cm square baking tray with baking
   parchment.

2. Mash the bananas and put them into a bowl with the
   eggs and vanilla extract. Mix well with a spoon.

3. Add the cooked quinoa, oats and raisins and mix again.
   Finally, stir in the chopped strawberries.

4. Transfer the mixture to the lined baking tray, smooth
   it down with the back of a spoon to make it level,
   then bake it in the oven for 20–25 minutes until firm
   to touch.

5. Remove from the oven and leave to cool, then cut
   into 9 squares.

6. The bars will keep in the fridge in an airtight container
   for up to 3 days or can be frozen for up to 3 months
   and defrosted at room temperature.

FRUIT AND NUT BREAKFAST COOKIES

| Makes: 6 cookies | Prep time: 10 minutes | Cook time: 15 minutes |

Sweetened with bananas and a little honey, and packed with nutritious ingredients and slow-releasing carbs and fibre, these breakfast cookies make a healthy start and are perfect for feeding your family on busy mornings. Serve with some yoghurt and chopped fresh fruit.

Ingredients

40g dried fruit (I use raisins, cherries, apricots and cranberries), chopped into small pieces

2 tbsp orange juice

2 medium ripe bananas, peeled and mashed

2 tbsp honey or maple syrup

100g rolled oats

30g chopped mixed nuts (I use pecans, walnuts, hazelnuts and flaked almonds)

2 tbsp plain flour

2 tbsp mixed seeds (I use a mix of sunflower, pumpkin, sesame and linseeds)

1 tbsp ground flaxseed

1 tbsp chia seeds

¼ tsp grated orange zest

Method

1. Preheat the oven to 180°C/160°C Fan/Gas Mark 4 and line a baking tray with baking parchment.

2. Put the chopped dried fruit into a small bowl and add the orange juice. Leave to soak for a few minutes.

3. Put the rest of the ingredients into a separate large bowl and mix well. Add the dried fruit and orange juice and mix again.

4. Divide the mixture evenly into 6 balls and place the balls on the lined baking tray. Press the balls down with the back of a spoon and use your hands to mould them into a 7-8cm cookie shape.

5. Bake for 15 minutes until they start to brown around the edges but are still soft.

6. Remove from the oven and leave to cool on a wire rack before serving.

OVERNIGHT OATS TWO WAYS

| Serves: 4 | Prep time: 2 minutes |

Overnight oats are probably the quickest and easiest breakfast you can make.
All the prep can be done the night before and you wake up
to an instant breakfast!

CHOCOLATE BANANA OVERNIGHT OATS

Ingredients

200g rolled oats

300ml milk

150g plain yoghurt

1 medium ripe banana, peeled and
mashed or chopped

1 tbsp cocoa powder

1 tbsp honey or maple syrup

Method

1. Mix all the ingredients together in a bowl or jar, cover
with cling film or foil and place in the fridge, preferably
overnight (or for at least 1 hour).

2. When you are ready to tuck in, remove from the fridge.
The oats can be eaten cold or heated in the microwave
for 30–60 seconds.

3. The oat mixture will keep, covered, in the fridge
for 2–3 days.

STRAWBERRY SHORTCAKE OVERNIGHT OATS

Ingredients

200g strawberries, hulled and
chopped

200g rolled oats

300ml milk

150g plain yoghurt

1 tbsp strawberry jam

½ tsp vanilla extract

Method

1. Mix all the ingredients together in a bowl or jar, cover
with cling film or foil and place in the fridge, preferably
overnight (or for at least 1 hour).

2. When you are ready to tuck in, remove from the fridge.
The oats can be eaten cold or heated in the microwave
for 30–60 seconds.

3. The oat mixture will keep, covered, in the fridge
for 2–3 days.

PORRIDGE BREAD

| Makes: 1 loaf | Prep time: 7 minutes | Cook time: 50 minutes |

If you love the idea of porridge for breakfast but your kids hate it, then this is a great alternative. By baking the oats with yoghurt, egg and milk you get a lovely rustic wholegrain bread that's delicious served with butter and jam or honey.

Ingredients

400g rolled oats

2 tsp bicarbonate of soda

½ tsp fine salt

500g plain yoghurt

50ml milk

1 egg, lightly beaten

2 tbsp mixed seeds (optional)

Method

1. Preheat the oven to 200°C/180°C Fan/Gas Mark 6. Grease a 900g (2lb) loaf tin and line it with baking parchment.

2. Mix the oats, bicarbonate of soda and salt together in a large bowl. Add the yoghurt, milk and beaten egg and mix again until well combined.

3. Pour the mixture into the tin, level it out with the back of a spoon and use a knife to draw a line down the middle of the loaf. Sprinkle the seeds on top, if using.

4. Bake in the oven for 45 minutes. Remove the bread from the tin and put it back into the oven, directly on the rack, for another 5 minutes. This will help to give the bread a more crispy crust.

5. Remove from the oven and leave to cool on a wire rack.

6. The bread will keep in an airtight container for up to 3 days.

BANANA AND BLUEBERRY LOAVES

| Makes: 10 mini loaves or muffins | Prep time: 10 minutes | Cook time: 20–25 minutes |

These filling mini loaves make the perfect breakfast to help keep
little tummies feeling full until lunchtime.

Ingredients

200g plain flour

75g rolled oats

1 tsp baking powder

¼ tsp bicarbonate of soda

½ tsp ground cinnamon

3 medium ripe bananas, peeled
and mashed

75g coconut oil or butter, melted,
plus extra for greasing (optional)

75g plain yoghurt

50g honey

1 egg

2 tsp vanilla extract

150g blueberries

Method

1. Preheat the oven to 200°C/180°C Fan/Gas Mark 6
   and put 10 greased mini loaf cases or muffin cases
   (or 10 paper loaf cases) on a baking tray.

2. Mix the flour, oats, baking powder, bicarbonate of soda
   and ground cinnamon together in a large bowl.

3. In a second bowl or jug mix the mashed bananas,
   coconut oil or butter, yoghurt, honey, egg and vanilla
   extract together, then add this mixture to the dry
   ingredients.

4. Mix gently with a spoon until well combined, then
   fold in the blueberries.

5. Divide the mixture evenly between the loaf or muffin
   cases and bake in the oven for 20–25 minutes until
   a skewer inserted into the middle of one of the loaves
   or muffins comes out clean.

6. Remove from the oven and leave to cool on a wire rack
   before serving.

7. These loaves will keep in an airtight container at room
   temperature for up to 3 days.

STRAWBERRY BANANA BREAD

| Makes: 1 loaf (about 8 slices) | Prep time: 10 minutes | Cook time: 1 hour |

A delicious and easy strawberry banana bread recipe, made even healthier as it contains no refined sugar. This makes the prefect sweet breakfast bread recipe, served with butter and some chopped fruit.

Ingredients

275g plain flour

1 tsp baking powder

¾ tsp bicarbonate of soda

2 medium ripe bananas, peeled and mashed

75g coconut oil or butter, melted, plus extra for greasing

75g honey

50g plain yoghurt

1 egg

2 tsp vanilla extract

100g strawberries, hulled and chopped

Method

1. Preheat the oven to 200°C/180°C Fan/Gas Mark 6. Grease a 900g (2lb) loaf tin with butter or oil then line it with baking parchment.

2. Put the flour, baking powder and bicarbonate of soda into a large bowl and mix with a spoon.

3. Put the mashed banana, melted coconut oil or butter, honey, yoghurt, egg and vanilla extract into a second bowl and mix well until combined.

4. Pour the wet ingredients into the bowl of dry ingredients and mix with a spoon, then fold in the chopped strawberries.

5. Transfer the mixture to the prepared loaf tin and bake in the oven for 20 minutes, then remove the tin from the oven, cover the bread loosely with foil, and return it to the oven. Turn the temperature down to 180°C/160°C Fan/Gas Mark 4 and bake for a further 35 minutes, or until a skewer inserted in the middle of the banana bread comes out clean.

6. Remove from the oven and leave to cool in the tin for 5-10 minutes before transferring to a wire rack to cool completely.

7. The loaf will keep well in an airtight container for up to 2 days, or can be sliced and frozen.

WEEKEND

Weekend breakfasts in your house are hopefully a little more leisurely than they are during the week, making them the perfect time to try something new and to get the kids involved in cooking. Many of these recipes are savoury, moving kids away from the idea that breakfast always has to involve something sweet.

Of course, if you have time mid-week to cook something from scratch then these are great breakfast options all week long.

VEGGIE EGG SCRAMBLE

| Serves: 2 | Prep time: 3 minutes | Cook time: 6 minutes |

Eggs are such a nutritious food, particularly during the winter months when children are more likely to be deficient in vitamin D.

Ingredients

½ tbsp butter

4 eggs

½ yellow pepper, finely chopped

100g cherry tomatoes, halved

30g fresh spinach

30g grated Cheddar cheese

salt and pepper, to taste

Method

1. Melt the butter in a frying pan over a medium heat and crack in the eggs. Mix them quickly with a wooden spoon or silicone spatula.

2. Cook the eggs for 1 minute, stirring constantly, then add the pepper, cherry tomatoes and spinach and cook for a further 3-4 minutes, stirring regularly.

3. Stir in the grated cheese and remove the pan from the heat. Season to taste and serve immediately.

SWEET POTATO HASH BROWNS

| Serves: 4 (makes 8 hash browns) | Prep time: 10 minutes | Cook time: 10–14 minutes |

A mixture of white and sweet potato creates a hash brown that's packed full of nutrients, especially when you leave the skins on. These are even better topped with a poached egg.

Ingredients

300g sweet potatoes, scrubbed

300g white potatoes, scrubbed

2 tbsp plain flour

¼ tsp garlic powder

2 tbsp olive or vegetable oil

salt and pepper, to taste

Method

1. Grate the potatoes into a large bowl and add the flour, garlic powder and a little salt and pepper. Mix well.

2. Heat the oil in a large frying pan over a medium heat. Use a spoon to transfer 4 portions of the mixture to the pan. Press down on each and fry for 3-4 minutes until crispy. Flip and fry on the other side for 2-3 minutes and transfer to a plate lined with kitchen paper. Cook the remaining mixture and serve immediately.

EGG AND SPINACH BREAKFAST POCKET

| Makes: 1 breakfast pocket | Prep time: 5 minutes | Cook time: 20 minutes |

Kids will love the novelty factor of these breakfast pockets. They're also great for teenagers who are always in a rush. Hand them one of these as they are heading out of the house in the morning and they can eat it on the go.

Ingredients

1 large tortilla wrap

35g fresh spinach

40g grated Cheddar cheese

1 egg

salt and pepper, to taste

Method

1. Preheat the oven to 200°C/180°C Fan/Gas Mark 6.

2. Lay the wrap on a square piece of foil that's bigger than the wrap and add the spinach in a small pile in the middle. Place the grated cheese on top of the spinach and make a small well in the middle. Crack the egg into the well and season with a little salt and pepper.

3. Fold the edges of the wrap over the mound of spinach, cheese and egg, enclosing the mound with the wrap, then wrap the pocket with the foil. Do not turn the pocket upside down or the egg will leak out!

4. Place on a baking tray and bake in the oven for 20 minutes. Remove from the oven, unwrap from the foil and allow the parcel to cool for a few minutes before serving.

BREAKFAST FRITTATA

GF BC

| Serves: 8 | Prep time: 3 minutes | Cook time: 28–30 minutes |

Frittata is a great way to make a delicious and nutritious egg breakfast for a crowd.
This recipe is packed full of lots of breakfast favourites like sausages and tomatoes.
It also keeps really well in the fridge to enjoy later in the week.

Ingredients

200g sausage meat or chopped, skinned sausages

120g cherry tomatoes, halved

1 garlic clove, crushed

6 eggs

1 spring onion, finely chopped

50g grated Cheddar cheese

½ tsp Dijon mustard

1 tbsp plain flour

Method

1. Preheat the oven to 200°C/180°C Fan/Gas Mark 6.

2. Put the sausage meat or chopped, skinned sausages, tomatoes and garlic into a baking dish (I use a 24cm dish) and bake in the oven for 10 minutes.

3. Crack the eggs into a jug and whisk with a fork. Add the spring onion, grated cheese, Dijon mustard and flour and mix well.

4. Remove the baking dish from the oven and pour the egg mixture on top of the sausages and tomatoes.

5. Put the dish back into the oven for a further 18-20 minutes until the frittata is firm to touch and is cooked through.

6. Remove from the oven and leave to cool a little before cutting into 8 slices.

7. The frittata will keep in an airtight container in the fridge for up to 3 days.

BEANS ON TOAST

| Serves: 4 | Prep time: 3 minutes | Cook time: 10 minutes |

Making your own baked beans at home is easier than you think. Use a tin or carton of cooked cannellini beans and in less than 15 minutes you will have a healthy beans-on-toast breakfast with a lot less sugar and salt than shop-bought baked beans.

Ingredients

1 tsp olive oil

1 shallot, finely chopped

1 garlic clove, crushed

300g passata

1 tbsp tomato purée

1 tsp Worcestershire sauce

1 tsp honey

½ tsp smoked paprika

¼ tsp dried mixed herbs

350g cooked cannellini beans from a tin or carton, drained

salt and pepper, to taste

4 slices of sourdough bread, to serve

Method

1. Heat the oil in a saucepan over a medium heat and add the chopped shallot. Fry for about 2 minutes until the onion has softened, then add the crushed garlic and fry for a further minute.

2. Add the passata, tomato purée, Worcestershire sauce, honey, smoked paprika and dried herbs and bring to the boil. Reduce the heat and simmer for 5 minutes.

3. Add the drained cannellini beans and cook for a further 2–3 minutes until the beans are warmed through.

4. Season to taste with salt and pepper and serve on toasted sourdough bread.

FRUITY PANCAKES

GF DF KM

| Serves: 4 (makes about 8 pancakes) | Prep time: 3 minutes | Cook time: 12 minutes |

Pancakes are a classic weekend breakfast and my Fruity Pancake
recipe uses only bananas to sweeten the batter.

Ingredients

2 medium ripe bananas

2 eggs

50g rolled oats

50g plain flour

25ml milk

pinch of ground cinnamon

150g mixed berries, roughly chopped

1 tbsp coconut oil

Method

1. Peel and mash the bananas in a bowl then add the eggs, oats, flour, milk and cinnamon. Mix well with a spoon. Fold in the berries.

2. Melt half the oil in a large frying pan over a medium heat. Using an ice cream scoop or spoon, heap the batter into the frying pan. You should be able to fit 4 pancakes in the pan at a time.

3. Fry the pancakes for about 3 minutes on each side until lightly browned.

4. Transfer the cooked pancakes to a plate. The pancakes will still be quite soft on the inside because of the fruit, but leave them to cool for a few minutes to firm up.

5. Meanwhile, melt the remaining oil in the pan and cook the rest of the batter, making another 4 pancakes.

HEALTHIER POP TARTS

| Makes: 8 pop tarts | Prep time: 12 minutes | Cook time: 18–20 minutes |

Who remembers eating pop tarts for breakfast as a kid? I used to love them, but they are not the most nutritious way to start the day. My version uses unsweetened pastry and healthier homemade fillings. Just as tasty, but a little better for the kids.

Ingredients

320g ready-rolled sheet
of shortcrust pastry

1 egg, lightly beaten

filling of your choice
(see below – each filling is enough
for one pop tart)

Banana, hazelnut and chocolate
⅓ banana, peeled and sliced

1 tbsp Chocolate-hazelnut Spread
(see page 183)

Raspberry jam
1 tbsp Raspberry Chia Jam (see
page 179) or your favourite jam

30g raspberries

Apple and cinnamon
2 tbsp Apple Sauce
(see page 186)

3 apple slices

pinch of ground cinnamon

Peanut butter and coconut
1 tbsp smooth peanut butter

1 tbsp coconut flakes

Method

1. Preheat the oven to 220°C/200°C Fan/Gas Mark 7 and line a baking tray with baking parchment.

2. Unroll the sheet of shortcrust pastry and cut it in half widthways so you now have 2 long rectangles. Cut each rectangle in half and then in half again so you end up with 8 pieces of pastry.

3. Place the fillings onto 4 pieces of pastry.

4. Using a pastry brush, brush each of the remaining 4 pieces of pastry with the beaten egg.

5. Place these pieces of pastry egg-side down onto the filling pieces of pastry and press down gently. Press the edges together with a fork and prick the top. Finally, brush the top with a little beaten egg.

6. Place the pop tarts onto the lined baking tray and bake in the oven for 18–20 minutes until golden brown.

7. Remove from the oven and leave the pop tarts to cool before serving as the fillings will be very hot.

CARAMELISED BANANA BREAKFAST PARFAIT

GF DF KM

| Serves: 4 | Prep time: 5 minutes | Cook time: 4—6 minutes |

A delicious breakfast parfait made with honey, caramelised bananas, Greek yoghurt, granola and cinnamon. Ideal for a Sunday morning!

Ingredients

4 medium bananas (not too ripe)

1 tbsp coconut oil

3 tbsp honey

400g plain Greek yoghurt

100g granola (see page 23 for my homemade granola)

pinch of ground cinnamon

Method

1. Cut the bananas into round 1.5cm-thick slices.

2. Melt the coconut oil in a frying pan over a medium heat and mix in 2 tablespoons of the honey. Add the banana slices so that each slice is sitting in the oil.

3. Fry gently for 2–3 minutes, or until the banana slices are starting to brown, then flip each banana slice and fry on the other side for a further 2–3 minutes. Remove the pan from the heat and leave to cool for a few minutes.

4. Build your parfait in bowls, glasses or cups, creating alternating layers of granola, caramelised banana and Greek yoghurt.

5. Drizzle with the remaining honey, add a sprinkle of cinnamon and serve.

LUNCH

QUICK AND EASY

Lunch at home can be so much more than a bland sandwich. With some simple ingredients and a few minutes you can whip up these delicious lunchtime treats for the whole family. Most of them can also be made in bulk and kept for several days in the fridge to serve up again another day.

CHICKEN AND VEGGIE FRITTATA FINGERS

| Serves: 4 | Prep time: 10 minutes | Cook time: 25 minutes |

A frittata makes a really great lunch for the whole family, either to eat
at home or to pack into lunchboxes for school and work.

Ingredients

200g frozen mixed chopped
vegetables or cooked vegetables

6 eggs

75g crème fraîche

100g cooked chicken, chopped

75g grated Cheddar cheese

1 tbsp plain flour

salt and pepper, to taste

Method

1. Preheat the oven to 200°C/180°C Fan/Gas Mark 6
   and line a baking dish with baking parchment (I use
   a 25cm square baking dish).

2. If using frozen vegetables, place them in a bowl, cover
   with boiling water and leave them for 3–4 minutes until
   they have defrosted and softened.

3. Meanwhile, crack the eggs into a large mixing bowl
   or jug and whisk gently with a fork. Add the crème
   fraîche, cooked chicken, grated cheese and flour
   and mix well. Season with a little salt and pepper.

4. Drain the vegetables well (if using frozen) and add
   them to the egg mixture.

5. Pour the frittata mixture into the prepared dish and
   bake in the oven for 25 minutes until the frittata is firm
   to touch.

6. Remove the frittata from the oven and allow it to cool
   for 10–15 minutes then cut into 8 large or 16 small slices.

7. These frittata slices will keep in the fridge, covered,
   for up to 2 days.

TORTILLA QUICHE

| Serves: 4 (makes 8 mini quiches) | Prep time: 7 minutes | Cook time: 15 minutes |

Homemade quiche usually requires a bit of time and patience but my quick and simple version uses tortilla wraps instead. Just as tasty but so much easier!

Ingredients

2 large tortilla wraps

4 large eggs

75g cooked vegetables, chopped, or chopped frozen vegetables (carrots, broccoli, peas, corn, etc.), defrosted

50g grated Cheddar cheese

40g ham, roughly chopped

1 tsp chopped chives

4 cherry tomatoes, halved

salt and pepper, to taste

Method

1. Preheat the oven to 200°C/180°C Fan/Gas Mark 6.

2. Use a 10cm cookie cutter or a plate of a similar size to cut out 4 circles from each tortilla (8 in total). Press the tortilla rounds into 8 holes of a muffin tray.

3. Crack the eggs into a large jug and whisk with a fork. Add the vegetables, grated cheese, ham and chives and mix well. Season with a little salt and pepper.

4. Divide the egg mixture between the 8 tortilla-lined muffin holes, and top each with a tomato half.

5. Bake in the oven for 15 minutes.

6. Remove from the oven and allow the quiches to cool for 5-10 minutes in the tray until fully set.

7. Serve immediately or keep in the fridge for up to 2 days.

BROCCOLI AND CHEESE QUESADILLA

| Serves: 2 | Prep time: 5 minutes | Cook time: 5 minutes |

I always think of a quesadilla as a Mexican-style toasted sandwich! It's a great way to sneak veggies into lunch. You can change up the recipe depending on what vegetables you have in the fridge.

Ingredients

150g cooked broccoli, chopped

75g grated Cheddar cheese

1 tbsp cream cheese

50g drained tinned sweetcorn

25g red pepper, chopped

2 large wholemeal tortilla wraps

salt and pepper, to taste

Method

1. Mix together the cooked broccoli, grated cheese, cream cheese, sweetcorn and red pepper in a large bowl. Season with a little salt and pepper.

2. Place one of the tortilla wraps in a large frying pan and spread the broccoli and cheese mixture on top, leaving just a small gap at the edge of the wrap.

3. Place the other wrap on top and press down gently.

4. Cook for 2 minutes over a low heat, being careful not to burn the wrap, then flip it over and cook for a further 1–2 minutes on the other side.

5. Remove the quesadilla from the frying pan and cut into 4, 6 or 8 triangles. Serve immediately.

TOASTIE PITTA POCKETS

| Serves: 2 | Prep time: 3 minutes | Cook time: 3 minutes |

Pitta breads are really handy to keep in the fridge and whip out for a quick and easy lunch. Pack them with your favourite fillings and pop them in the toaster to heat up!

Ingredients

2 mini pitta breads

filling of your choice (see below)

Ham and cheese
2 thick slices of ham

4 slices of cheese

Tuna, mayo and corn
120g tin tuna in water or brine (I use ½ a tin)

1 tbsp mayonnaise

2 tbsp drained tinned sweetcorn

BLT
4 slices of cooked bacon

2 lettuce leaves

1 sliced tomato

1 tbsp mayonnaise

Method

1. Put the mini pittas in the toaster for 30–40 seconds just to puff them up a little.

2. Remove them from the toaster and, using a sharp knife, make an incision across the top of each pitta bread.

3. Stuff the pitta with your chosen filling, and if you want to heat the pitta further, pop it back into the toaster for a further 1–2 minutes.

4. Serve immediately.

TUNA BITES

| Serves: 4 (makes 8 patties) | Prep time: 10 minutes | Cook time: 8 minutes |

Tinned tuna has quite a strong taste and smell but I find that by cooking it with a few other ingredients you can make it a lot more palatable for kids.

Ingredients

1 tbsp sesame oil

2 eggs

2 spring onions, finely chopped

1 garlic clove, crushed

200g frozen mixed chopped vegetables

250g cooked rice

150g cooked chicken, ham, prawns or salmon, chopped

1 tbsp light soy sauce

½ tbsp fish sauce

Method

1. Heat half the oil in a wok over a medium heat and crack in the eggs. Cook for 2–3 minutes, stirring constantly, until the eggs have scrambled, then transfer them to a bowl.

2. Heat the remaining oil in the wok and add the spring onions, garlic and frozen vegetables. Cook for 4–5 minutes, stirring regularly, until the vegetables are cooked through. Transfer them to the bowl with the eggs.

3. Add the cooked rice to the wok, along with the cooked chicken, ham, prawns or salmon, soy sauce and fish sauce and stir-fry for 2–3 minutes until the rice is hot.

4. Put the rest of the ingredients back into the wok and cook for a further minute, stirring well.

5. Serve immediately or keep in an airtight container in the fridge for up to 2 days.

TOMATO AND LENTIL SOUP WITH PARMESAN CRISPS

| Serves: 4 | Prep time: 10 minutes | Cook time: 50 minutes |

There's nothing better than a warming mug of soup on a cold winter's day.
The lentils in this soup make it really filling and add a nutritional
boost of protein and fibre. Serve it with the delicious
Parmesan crisps for dipping!

Ingredients

For the soup

½ tbsp olive oil

1 medium onion, finely diced

2 garlic cloves, crushed

1 medium carrot, finely diced

1 celery stick, finely diced

1 red pepper, halved, deseeded
and chopped

1 tsp smoked paprika

700ml vegetable stock

100g red lentils

400g tin plum tomatoes

1 tbsp tomato purée

For the Parmesan crisps

50g finely grated Parmesan cheese

Method

1. Heat the oil in a large saucepan over a medium heat, add the onion and fry for 2–3 minutes until soft.

2. Add the garlic, carrot, celery and pepper and fry for another couple of minutes, then add the smoked paprika and stir well.

3. Pour in about 600ml of the stock, together with the lentils, plum tomatoes and tomato purée and stir well. Bring the soup to the boil, then reduce the heat and simmer for 30–40 minutes.

4. Meanwhile, make the Parmesan crisps. Preheat the oven to 200°C/180°C Fan/Gas Mark 6 and line a baking tray with baking parchment.

5. Spoon little piles (about ½ tablespoon each) of grated Parmesan cheese onto the lined baking tray, then press them down so that they are an even thickness: you should have about 18 piles in total.

6. Bake in the oven for 5 minutes until the piles are crisp around the edges then remove from the oven and leave them to cool for 5 minutes to firm up.

7. Remove the soup from the heat and use a hand-held blender or a stand blender to blitz the soup to your desired consistency. If it seems too thick add a little of the remaining stock.

8. Serve the soup immediately, with the Parmesan crisps, or allow to cool and store in an airtight container in the fridge for up to 4 days. The soup can also be frozen for up to 3 months.

CHEESY CHICKEN FRITTERS

| Serves: 4 (makes 8 fritters) | Prep time: 7 minutes | Cook time: 16–20 minutes |

My daughter isn't a massive fan of chicken but she loves these cheesy chicken fritters. They make the perfect finger food for lunch served with some raw veggies on the side.

Ingredients

2 eggs

100g cream cheese

60g grated Cheddar cheese

50g plain flour

1 tbsp chopped chives

350g skinless chicken breasts, cut into small pieces

1 tbsp olive or vegetable oil

salt and pepper, to taste

crisp lettuce leaves, to serve

crème fraîche, to serve

Method

1. Mix together the eggs, cream cheese, grated cheese, flour and chives in a large bowl. Add the chopped chicken and season with salt and pepper.

2. Heat the oil in a large frying pan over a medium heat. Use an ice cream scoop or spoon to transfer 4 portions of the chicken mixture to the frying pan. Press down with a spatula and cook each fritter for 4-5 minutes on each side until they are cooked through.

3. Transfer the fritters to a plate lined with kitchen paper and cook the remaining fritters.

4. Serve immediately, in lettuce 'cups', with crème fraîche for dipping, or leave to cool at room temperature.

5. The fritters will keep in an airtight container in the fridge for up to 2 days.

FREEZER FRIENDLY

If you like to get ahead by preparing school and work lunches in advance,
then these recipes are ideal for making in bulk and storing in the
freezer for busy days. They also make great finger food
for kiddie parties and play dates.

CHEESE AND CHIVE ROLLS

| Makes: 8 large or 16 small rolls | Prep time: 15 minutes | Cook time: 18–20 minutes |

These rolls make a great veggie alternative to sausage rolls and
are packed with spinach. Shhh, don't tell the kids!

Ingredients

150g breadcrumbs, homemade
  or shop-bought

50g fresh spinach

100g grated Cheddar cheese

25g grated Parmesan cheese

1 shallot, finely diced

1 tbsp chopped chives

1 tsp Dijon mustard

320g ready-rolled sheet
  of puff pastry

1 egg, beaten

½ tsp poppy seeds or sesame
  seeds (optional)

Method

1. Preheat the oven to 200°C/180°C Fan/Gas Mark 6
   and line a baking sheet with baking parchment.

2. Put the breadcrumbs and spinach into a food processor
   and blitz for 1 minute until the spinach has substantially
   reduced in volume.

3. Add the grated cheeses, shallot, chives and mustard and
   blitz once again until all the ingredients have combined.

4. Unroll the sheet of pastry and cut it in half lengthways
   so that you have 2 rectangles. Divide the spinach and
   cheese mixture in half and spread it along the length
   of each pastry sheet, down the middle, leaving
   a gap of about 1cm on either side.

5. Fold the pastry over the mixture so that the edges meet
   and press down on the edges with a fork to seal the rolls.

6. Cut each of the two long rolls into 8, giving you 16 small
   rolls in total (or make 8 larger rolls if you prefer). Place the
   cheese and chive rolls on the lined baking sheet and brush
   them with a little beaten egg. Sprinkle some poppy or
   sesame seeds on top, if using.

7. Bake in the oven for 18-20 minutes until golden brown
   and cooked through. Remove from the oven and leave
   to cool a little on the baking sheet before serving.

8. The rolls will keep in the fridge for up to 3 days. To freeze,
   place the uncooked rolls (without the egg wash or seeds)
   in a single layer on a tray or plate. Freeze until solid then
   transfer to a freezer bag or container. To cook from frozen,
   brush with a little beaten egg, sprinkle with seeds and bake
   as above, adding a few more minutes to the cooking time.

HIDDEN VEGGIE SAUSAGE ROLLS

| Makes: 8 large or 16 small rolls | Prep time: 15 minutes | Cook time: 35 minutes |

Most kids love sausage rolls, so I like to sneak some veggies into mine. These are great for lunchboxes and brilliant for parties and play dates, too.

Ingredients

1 tsp olive or vegetable oil

1 medium courgette, grated

1 large carrot, grated

1 garlic clove, crushed or finely chopped

350g sausage meat

320g ready-rolled sheet of puff pastry

1 egg, beaten

½ tbsp poppy seeds or sesame seeds (optional)

Method

1. Preheat the oven to 200°C/180°C Fan/Gas Mark 6 and line a baking sheet with baking parchment.

2. Heat the oil in a frying pan over a low heat, add the grated courgette, carrot and garlic and cook for about 4 minutes until the vegetables are soft but not browned.

3. Transfer the cooked vegetables to a large bowl along with the sausage meat and mix well.

4. While the mixture is cooling, unroll the sheet of pastry and cut it in half lengthways so that you have 2 rectangles.

5. Divide the sausage meat mixture in half and spread it along the length of each piece of pastry, down the middle, leaving a gap of about 1cm on either side.

6. Fold the pastry over the sausage meat mixture so that the edges meet and press down on the edges with a fork to seal the rolls.

7. Cut each of the two long rolls into 4 to make 8 large sausage rolls (or make 16 small ones if you prefer). Place the sausage rolls on the lined baking sheet and brush them with a little beaten egg. Sprinkle some poppy or sesame seeds on top, if using.

8. Bake in the oven for 25–35 minutes until golden brown and cooked through (the cooking time will depend on the size of the sausage rolls so check them often from 25 minutes). Remove from the oven and leave to cool for a few minutes on the baking sheet before serving.

9. The sausage rolls are best eaten on the day they are baked but they will keep in the fridge for up to 3 days. To freeze, follow the instructions on page 61.

VEGGIE PIZZA ROLL-UPS

| Serves: 8 | Prep time: 5 minutes | Cook time: 15 minutes |

Super-easy to make and packed with mixed vegetables, these veggie pizza puff pastry roll-ups are sure to go down a treat with the whole family.

Ingredients

150g frozen mixed chopped vegetables (or cooked fresh chopped vegetables)

320g ready-rolled sheet of puff pastry

75g tomato purée or tomato sauce

100g grated Cheddar cheese

1 egg, beaten

½ tsp dried oregano

Method

1. Preheat the oven to 220°C/200°C Fan/Gas Mark 7 and line 2 baking trays with baking parchment.

2. Put the veg (if using frozen) in a large microwavable bowl or jug, cover with boiling water and cook for 1 minute in the microwave. Drain and transfer to kitchen paper to absorb as much water as possible.

3. Unroll the pastry and spread the tomato purée or sauce on top. Sprinkle over the cheese and finally add the cooked vegetables.

4. Starting with the shorter edge of the pastry sheet, roll the pastry up, keeping it as tight and compact as possible, then cut it into 8 pieces and divide them between the lined trays.

5. Brush with a little egg wash, sprinkle over the oregano and bake in the oven for 15 minutes until the pastry is golden brown.

6. Remove from the oven and leave the rolls to cool a little before eating so that they keep their shape.

7. To freeze ahead, place the 8 uncooked roll-ups in a single layer on a tray or plate and freeze until solid. Transfer to a freezer bag or container and keep in the freezer for up to 6 months. They can be cooked from frozen but add a few more minutes to the cooking time.

CAULIFLOWER CHEESE CAKES

| Serves: 4 (makes 8 cakes) | Prep time: 15 minutes | Cook time: 12 minutes |

All the delicious taste of cauliflower cheese packed together with mashed potato to make a really tasty lunchtime treat. These are ideal to make at the weekend and keep in the fridge or freezer for later in the week.

Ingredients

350g white potatoes, peeled and cut into small chunks

350g cauliflower, cut into small chunks

1 vegetable stock cube

50g grated Cheddar cheese

20g grated Parmesan cheese

1 spring onion, finely diced

1 garlic clove, crushed

1 egg

3 tbsp plain flour

1 tsp wholegrain mustard

1 tbsp olive or vegetable oil

salt and pepper, to taste

crème fraîche, to serve

Method

1. Put the chunks of potato and cauliflower into a large saucepan, crumble in the stock cube and cover with boiling water. Bring to the boil, then reduce the heat and simmer for 8-10 minutes until the potato and cauliflower chunks are soft. Remove from the heat and drain well.

2. Put the drained potato and cauliflower back into the saucepan (off the heat) and mash with a potato masher (it's fine to leave a few small lumps for added texture). Add the cheeses, spring onion, garlic, egg, flour and mustard and mix thoroughly with a spoon until well combined. Season with a little salt and pepper.

3. Heat the oil in a large frying pan over a medium heat. Using an ice cream scoop or spoon, put 4 separate heaped spoonfuls of the mash mixture into the pan. Push down with a spatula and cook for about 3 minutes on each side until golden brown.

4. Transfer to a plate lined with kitchen paper and repeat with the rest of the mixture. Serve immediately with a dollop of crème fraîche.

5. If making ahead, store in an airtight container in the fridge for up to 2 days or freeze the cooked and cooled cakes, individually wrapped in foil or baking parchment, then place in a freezer bag or container. Defrost in the fridge overnight and reheat them in the oven or microwave.

SPINACH AND CHEESE MUFFINS

  BC

| Serves: 12 | Prep time: 5 minutes | Cook time: 20–25 minutes |

Delicious savoury muffins packed full of vegetables; perfect to pop into lunchboxes or for an afternoon snack. You can replace the spinach and peppers with other leftover cooked vegetables such as carrots, broccoli and peas.

Ingredients

2 eggs

150ml milk

75g butter, melted

150g grated Cheddar cheese

1 spring onion, finely chopped

75g fresh baby spinach, chopped

½ red pepper, diced

250g self-raising flour

½ vegetable stock cube

salt and pepper, to taste

Method

1. Preheat the oven to 200°C/180°C Fan/Gas Mark 6 and line a muffin tray with 12 muffin cases.

2. Gently whisk the eggs in a large bowl and stir in the milk and melted butter. Mix in the grated cheese, spring onion, baby spinach and diced pepper. Finally, add the flour, crumble in the stock cube and season with a little salt and pepper. Mix gently until all the ingredients are combined.

3. Divide the mixture between the 12 muffin cases and bake in the oven for 20-25 minutes until cooked through (a skewer inserted into the middle of one of the muffins should come out clean).

4. Remove from the oven and leave to cool in the muffin tray for a few minutes, then transfer to a wire rack to cool completely.

5. The muffins will keep in the fridge for up to 3 days and can be reheated in the microwave or oven, or can be frozen. Freeze the cooled muffins in a single layer on a tray or plate then transfer to a freezer bag or container. To defrost, simply leave out at room temperature for a few hours or overnight, then eat at room temperature or warm them in the microwave.

LUNCHBOX IDEAS

Packing school lunches can cause a lot of stress for parents. It's not easy juggling a fussy-eating child's tastes with the healthy-foods-only policy that most schools now have in place. I know my daughter loves nothing more than a plain ham sandwich in her lunchbox but if you want to shake up your lunchtime repertoire a bit, here are some ideas that your kids might enjoy.

Making food appealing to children is half the battle when is comes to fussy eating. Use fun lunchboxes and coloured pots and skewers, along with vibrant fruit and veg to make a lunch that's exciting and inviting to kids as well as being filling and healthy. I've used a mix of recipes from this book along with some other simple but fun food ideas such as sausage skewers and stuffed mini deli peppers. Don't be afraid to get creative with your own ideas!

SPINACH AND CHEESE MUFFIN LUNCHBOX
- Spinach and Cheese Muffin (see page 67)
- Handful of rice cakes
- Chopped veggies and fruit
- Energy Bites (made with sunflower butter) (see page 128)

SAUSAGE ROLL LUNCHBOX
- Hidden Veggie Sausage Rolls (see page 62)
- Cheesy Cheddar Crackers (see page 151)
- Chopped veggies and fruit
- Yoghurt

VEGGIE RICE LUNCHBOX
- Savoury Veggie Rice (see page 117)
- Pieces of cheese on skewers
- Chopped veggies and fruit
- Fruity Flapjack (see page 127)

TORTILLA QUICHE LUNCHBOX
- Tortilla Quiche (see page 50)
- Seeded Oatcakes (see page 150)
- Chopped veggies and fruit
- Carrot and Orange Greek Yoghurt Muffin (see page 135)

TURKEY SALAD WRAP LUNCHBOX
- Turkey or chicken slices, lettuce, tomato and avocado mayo wrap
- Piece of cheese
- Chopped veggies and fruit
- Slice of Strawberry Banana Bread (see page 33)

SAUSAGE SKEWERS LUNCHBOX
- Mini sausages and tomatoes on skewers
- Garlic and Herb Breadsticks (see page 153)
- Hummus or any other dip
- Chopped veggies and fruit
- Raspberry Chia Crumble Square (see page 163)

CHEESY CHICKEN FRITTERS LUNCHBOX
- Cheesy Chicken Fritters (see page 59)
- Mini deli peppers stuffed with cream cheese
- Chopped veggies and fruit
- Cranberry and Coconut Cookie (see page 133)

HAM, CHEESE AND APPLE LETTUCE WRAP LUNCHBOX
- Ham, cheese and apple lettuce wrap
- A few tortilla chips
- Hummus or any other dip
- Chopped veggies and fruit
- Handful of popcorn

FAMILY MEALS

PASTA, RICE AND NOODLES

Pasta- and rice-based dishes are staple evening meals in our house. They tend to be tried and tested recipes that I know I can whip up quickly and that everyone will eat with minimal fuss. Most of these recipes are also veggie-packed, ideal for getting maximum nutrients into your picky eaters!

The pasta sauce recipes are brilliant to make in bulk and keep in the freezer for another day.

CREAMY ROASTED PEPPER PASTA SAUCE

| Serves: 4 | Prep time: 3 minutes | Cook time: 35 minutes |

A no-fuss pasta sauce that's super-easy to make. The vegetables are roasted in the oven and then blitzed up in a blender. Minimal effort but maximum taste!

Ingredients

400g red peppers, halved, deseeded and roughly chopped

400g vine tomatoes

1 ½ tbsp olive oil

½ tsp dried oregano

2 garlic cloves, peeled but left whole

250g dried pasta

75g cream cheese

20g grated Parmesan cheese

Method

1. Preheat the oven to 220°C/200°C Fan/Gas Mark 7.

2. Put the peppers on a large baking tray. Cut the tomatoes in half and add them to the tray. Drizzle over the oil and add the dried oregano and garlic. Mix well.

3. Roast in the oven for 30 minutes, stirring once.

4. Meanwhile, cook the pasta in a large saucepan according to the packet instructions, then drain.

5. Remove the vegetables from the oven and add them to a stand blender or food processor. Blitz until smooth, then add the cream cheese and Parmesan and blitz again.

6. Mix the sauce with the cooked pasta and serve immediately.

7. Keep any leftover sauce in an airtight container in the fridge for up to 3 days or freeze for up to 3 months.

SESAME CHICKEN NOODLES

| Serves: 4 | Prep time: 5 minutes | Cook time: 11–15 minutes |

A delicious but super-simple family meal of sesame-honey chicken
and vegetable noodles. Ready in just 15 minutes!

Ingredients

½ tbsp sesame oil

300g skinless chicken breasts, diced

1 red pepper, halved, deseeded
and diced

2 spring onions, chopped

1 carrot, shaved into long strips
with a vegetable peeler

2 garlic cloves, crushed

150g dried egg noodles

100ml chicken stock

1½ tbsp cornflour

2 tbsp honey

3 tbsp soy sauce

100g mixture of frozen peas
and sweetcorn

½ tbsp sesame seeds

Method

1. Heat the oil in a wok over a medium heat and add the
diced chicken. Fry for 7–10 minutes until the chicken
has just about cooked through, then add the red
pepper, spring onions, carrot shavings and crushed
garlic and cook for 2–3 minutes, stirring regularly.

2. Meanwhile cook the egg noodles in another saucepan
according to the packet instructions.

3. In a small jug or cup mix the chicken stock and cornflour
together well and add it to the wok along with the
honey and soy sauce. Add the frozen peas and
sweetcorn and cook for another couple of minutes
until the sauce has thickened.

4. Drain the noodles and add them to the wok, mixing
them well with the chicken, vegetables and sauce.

5. Serve immediately with a sprinkling of sesame seeds
on top.

POPEYE'S PROTEIN PESTO

| Serves: 6 | Prep time: 2 minutes |

The combination of peas, spinach and seeds means this pesto packs a powerful nutritional punch and it doesn't require any cooking! I prefer to use a light and mild olive oil as extra virgin olive oil can be too strong for little taste buds.

Ingredients

150g frozen peas

75g fresh spinach

5–7 basil leaves

50g grated Parmesan cheese

1 garlic clove, crushed

1 tbsp sesame seeds

1 tbsp pumpkin seeds

1 tbsp sunflower seeds

juice of ½ lemon

120ml light and mild olive oil

salt and pepper, to taste

Method

1. Put the frozen peas and spinach in a food processor and blitz until the spinach has broken down.

2. Add the basil, Parmesan, garlic, seeds and lemon juice and blitz again until well combined.

3. Slowly drizzle in the olive oil through the funnel while the blade is still turning, until the pesto is as smooth as possible. Season to taste with salt and pepper and serve with cooked pasta or as a dip for Breadsticks (see page 153). It can also be used to make Pesto Pastry Straws (see page 148).

4. This pesto can be kept in an airtight container in the fridge for up to 5 days or frozen and kept in the freezer for up to 3 months.

BATCH-COOK BOLOGNESE

| Serves: 8 | Prep time: 10 minutes | Cook time: 1 hour 10 minutes |

Spag bol is a classic family favourite. My recipe makes eight portions,
so it's ideal to pack away in the freezer for those busy days when
you have no time to cook a dish from scratch.

Ingredients

150g smoked bacon lardons

1 large onion, finely diced

3 medium carrots, diced

2 celery sticks, diced

2 garlic cloves, crushed

1kg minced beef

400g tin chopped tomatoes

150ml beef stock, plus extra,
   if needed

100ml red wine (or more beef stock)

4 tbsp tomato purée

1 tsp dried Italian herbs

Method

1. Place a large frying pan or casserole dish over a medium heat, add the bacon lardons and fry for 4–5 minutes until crispy. Transfer them to a bowl but keep as much of the bacon fat as possible in the pan.

2. Add the onion to the pan and cook for 2–3 minutes until soft, then add the carrots, celery and garlic and fry for a further 2 minutes. Add the minced beef and cook until brown, breaking it up with a wooden spoon.

3. Tip in the chopped tomatoes, beef stock and red wine and mix well. Add the tomato purée and dried herbs, along with the cooked bacon lardons and stir again.

4. Bring the bolognese to the boil, then reduce the heat and simmer for 1 hour. If the bolognese gets too dry, add some extra beef stock.

5. Remove from the heat and serve with cooked pasta or spaghetti.

6. Keep the rest in an airtight container in the fridge for up to 2 days or in the freezer for up to 3 months. Defrost at room temperature, or overnight in the fridge, and reheat in a saucepan over a medium heat.

SMOKY MEATBALL PASTA BAKE

GF BC

| Serves: 4 | Prep time: 15 minutes | Cook time: 25 minutes |

There's something really comforting about homemade meatballs and pasta. This is one of my family's favourite meals and I hope it becomes one of yours, too.

Ingredients

500g minced beef

1 shallot, finely diced

1 garlic clove, crushed

60g breadcrumbs

1 egg

1 tsp dried Italian herbs

1 tsp oil or spray oil

250g dried pasta

500g passata

75ml red wine or beef stock

1 tbsp Worcestershire sauce

1 tsp smoked paprika

40g grated Cheddar cheese

30g grated mozzarella

salt and pepper, to taste

Method

1. Preheat the oven to 200°C/180°C Fan/Gas Mark 6.

2. Start by making the meatballs. Put the minced beef, shallot, garlic, breadcrumbs, egg and dried herbs in a bowl and mix well with your hands. Form the mixture into 12 meatballs.

3. Lightly grease a large baking dish with oil or spray oil and place the meatballs in it. Bake them in the oven for 15 minutes.

4. Meanwhile, cook the pasta in a large pan of boiling water according to the packet instructions.

5. When the pasta has cooked, drain it. Remove the meatballs from the oven after 15 minutes and add the pasta to that dish.

6. In a large jug mix the passata, red wine or beef stock, Worcestershire sauce and smoked paprika. Pour this sauce over the meatballs and pasta and top with grated Cheddar and mozzarella. Return the dish to the oven to bake for 10 minutes.

7. Remove from the oven and serve immediately with some green veggies or salad. Leftovers can be kept in an airtight container in the fridge for up to 2 days.

MEAL PLAN

HIDDEN VEGGIE TOMATO SAUCE

| Serves: 10 | Prep time: 10 minutes | Cook time: 25 minutes |

Got a veggie-hating family? Try my hidden veggie tomato sauce, which is perfect for pastas and pizzas, has no added sugar and can be frozen, too! If your kids really hate the sight of any green, leave out the fresh basil leaves.

Ingredients

1 tbsp olive oil

1 medium onion, finely diced

2 garlic cloves, crushed

3 carrots, finely diced

2 celery sticks, finely diced

2 courgettes, finely diced

1 red pepper, halved, deseeded and chopped

500ml vegetable stock

1.5kg passata

1 tbsp tomato purée

1 tsp dried Italian herbs

1 tsp smoked paprika

handful of fresh basil leaves (optional)

Method

1. Heat the oil in a large saucepan over a medium heat, add the onion and fry for 2–3 minutes, then add the garlic and fry for another minute before adding the carrot, celery, courgette and red pepper.

2. Pour in the stock and passata and stir well. Add the tomato purée, dried herbs and smoked paprika and bring to the boil, then reduce the heat and simmer for about 20 minutes, or until the vegetables are soft. If you want to add the fresh basil leaves, do so once the vegetables are soft.

3. Remove from the heat and blitz the sauce either with a hand-held blender or in a stand blender until smooth. Be careful as it will be very hot! If the sauce is too thick, simply add some extra vegetable stock or water to thin it down.

4. Use as a pasta sauce or on pizzas, and pour the remaining sauce into jars, containers or freezer bags and allow to cool before chilling or freezing. The sauce will keep in the fridge for up to 4 days and in the freezer for up to 3 months. After defrosting, add some vegetable stock or water if it's too thick.

SEVEN VEG LENTIL LASAGNE

| Serves: 6 | Prep time: 10 minutes | Cook time: 45 minutes |

This veggie-packed lasagne is a great way to get several portions of veg into your family in just one sitting. The white sauce is no-cook, using crème fraîche instead, to save some time and unnecessary washing up!

Ingredients

1 tbsp olive oil

1 medium onion, finely diced

2 garlic cloves, crushed

2 carrots, finely diced

2 celery sticks, finely diced

1 courgette, chopped

1 red pepper, halved, deseeded and chopped

150g red lentils

500ml vegetable stock, plus extra

400g tin chopped tomatoes

2 tbsp tomato purée

1 tbsp fresh herb leaves (I use oregano, thyme and rosemary)

½ tsp smoked paprika

75g frozen peas

75g frozen or tinned sweetcorn

50g frozen or fresh spinach

250g dried lasagne sheets

100g crème fraîche

60g grated Cheddar cheese

20g grated Parmesan cheese

Method

1. Heat the oil in a large saucepan over a medium heat, add the onion and fry for 2-3 minutes until soft, then add the garlic, carrots, celery, courgette and red pepper and fry for a further 2 minutes. Add the lentils, vegetable stock, tinned tomatoes, tomato purée, herbs and smoked paprika. Bring to the boil, then reduce the heat and simmer for 20 minutes, or until the lentils are just cooked.

2. Add the peas, sweetcorn and spinach and cook for a few minutes until the spinach has wilted. If the mixture becomes too dry at any point add some extra stock. Remove from the heat.

3. Preheat the oven to 200°C/180°C Fan/Gas Mark 6. Using a large baking dish (I use a 24cm square dish) layer the lasagne sheets with the lentil filling until both are used up, finishing with a layer of lasagne sheets. Spoon the crème fraîche on top then sprinkle over the grated cheeses.

4. Bake in the oven for 15-20 minutes until a knife easily goes through the lasagne sheets.

5. Remove from the oven and serve immediately, either on its own or with a side of vegetables, or allow to cool and keep covered in the fridge for up to 3 days. The lasagne can also be divided into portions and frozen. Allow to defrost fully in the fridge, then heat in the microwave or in the oven.

CHICKEN, CHORIZO AND PRAWN PAELLA

GF   DF   BC

| Serves: 4 | Prep time: 5 minutes | Cook time: 25–30 minutes |

This delicious paella recipe is so easy to make yet packed full of flavour.
It's a great to dish to make mid-week when you need to get a simple
but tasty meal on the table fast. One-pot cooking made easy!

Ingredients

½ tbsp olive oil

50g chorizo, roughly diced

350g skinless, boneless chicken
   thighs, roughly chopped

1 small onion, diced

2 garlic cloves, crushed

1 red pepper, halved, deseeded
   and diced

250g paella rice

½ tsp smoked paprika

½ tsp dried rosemary

pinch of saffron or turmeric

1 litre vegetable or chicken stock

100g frozen prawns

100g frozen peas

lemon wedges, to serve

Method

1. Heat the oil in a large frying pan over a medium heat.
   Add the chorizo and chicken thighs and fry for
   4-5 minutes until the chicken is browned. Then
   transfer to a bowl.

2. Add the onion to the same pan and fry for 2-3 minutes
   until it starts to soften, then add the garlic and red
   pepper and fry for a further 2 minutes.

3. Return the chorizo and chicken thighs to the pan, along
   with the paella rice, smoked paprika, dried rosemary,
   saffron or turmeric and stock. Stir well, bring to the boil,
   then reduce the heat and simmer for about 15 minutes
   until the rice is just about cooked.

4. Add the frozen prawns and peas and cook for a futher
   3 minutes, then remove from the heat and serve
   immediately with lemon wedges on the side.

5. This paella can be kept covered in the fridge for
   up to 2 days.

MEAL PLAN

HIDDEN VEGGIE RISOTTO

GF FR BC

| Serves: 4 | Prep time: 10 minutes | Cook time: 25 minutes |

This recipe is perfect for kids that like rice-based dishes but are not so keen on veggies.
It contains four different types of nutritious vegetables all mixed
into a creamy and cheesy risotto.

Ingredients

200g carrots, chopped

200g butternut squash, peeled
and chopped

150g sweet potato, peeled
and chopped

150g cauliflower, cut into
small florets

100ml milk

1 tbsp butter

1 tsp olive oil

1 small onion, finely diced

250g risotto rice

1 litre hot vegetable stock

50g grated Parmesan cheese

Method

1. Put the carrots, butternut squash, sweet potato and
   cauliflower into a large saucepan, cover with boiling
   water and cook over a medium heat for 7–9 minutes,
   or until all the vegetables are soft.

2. Drain the vegetables and add them to a food processor
   or stand blender with the milk and butter and blitz
   until smooth.

3. Heat the oil in a large saucepan, add the onion and
   fry for 2–3 minutes until soft.

4. Add the risotto rice and cook for a further couple
   of minutes, stirring constantly.

5. Keep the stock in a pan or jug beside the pan. Add
   a couple of ladles of stock to the rice and cook, stirring,
   until the stock has been absorbed, then continue
   adding ladlefuls of stock – a couple at a time – for about
   15 minutes until the rice is cooked al dente (you may not
   need all the stock).

6. Once the rice is ready, remove the pan from the heat
   and stir in the blitzed vegetables. Finally, stir in the
   grated Parmesan.

7. Serve immediately. Leftovers will keep, covered
   in the fridge, for up to 3 days or can be frozen
   for up to 3 months. Defrost at room temperature,
   or overnight in the fridge and reheat in the
   microwave or on the hob.

MEAL PLAN

CHEESE AND TOMATO BAKED RISOTTO

| Serves: 4 | Prep time: 3 minutes | Cook time: 35 minutes |

A delicious and kid-friendly cheese and tomato risotto recipe, cooked
in the oven to make it super-easy. Serve it up with
some cooked greens or a side salad.

Ingredients

1 tbsp olive oil

1 onion, finely diced

2 garlic cloves, chopped

250g cherry tomatoes

250g risotto rice

750ml vegetable stock

75g grated Cheddar cheese

1 tbsp chopped chives

Method

1. Preheat the oven to 220°C/200°C Fan/Gas Mark 7.

2. Put the olive oil, onion, garlic and tomatoes in a baking dish and bake in the oven for 15 minutes.

3. After 15 minutes the tomatoes will be nicely roasted: either leave them whole or gently mash them to break them down.

4. Add the risotto rice and vegetable stock to the dish and return to the oven for a further 20 minutes, stirring the rice twice, until the rice has absorbed all the stock and is cooked through.

5. Remove from the oven, stir in the grated cheese and chives and serve immediately.

6. Leftovers can be kept covered in the fridge for up to 3 days or can be frozen for up to 3 months.

FRUITY VEGGIE CURRY

   GF DF FR BC

| Serves: 4 | Prep time: 10 minutes | Cook time: 25 minutes |

My fruity curry is mild enough for little taste buds but still packed full of flavour and made deliciously sweet with carrots and mango chutney.

Ingredients

½ tbsp vegetable or sunflower oil

1 onion, finely diced

1 garlic clove, crushed

250g butternut squash, peeled and cut into 2cm dice

2 medium carrots, roughly chopped

½ tbsp medium curry powder

1 tbsp tomato purée

500ml vegetable stock

1 tbsp mango chutney

200g basmati rice

1 medium apple, peeled, cored and roughly chopped

1 small courgette, roughly chopped

150g drained tinned chickpeas

25g raisins

50g frozen peas

50g fresh or frozen spinach

Method

1. Heat the oil in a large saucepan over a medium heat, add the onion and fry for 2–3 minutes until soft.

2. Add the garlic, butternut squash and carrots and fry for a further 2 minutes, then stir in the curry powder, tomato purée, vegetable stock and mango chutney and mix well. Bring to the boil, then reduce the heat, cover and simmer for about 10 minutes.

3. While the curry is cooking, cook the rice in another pan according to the packet instructions.

4. Add the apple, courgette, chickpeas and raisins to the curry, cover and cook for a further 5 minutes. Finally, add the peas and spinach and cook for 2–3 minutes until the spinach has wilted.

5. Serve immediately with the rice.

6. The curry will keep in an airtight container in the fridge for up to 2 days, or in the freezer for up to 3 months. Defrost at room temperature, or overnight in the fridge, and reheat in a saucepan over a medium heat.

MEAT

Lots of parents struggle to get their kids to eat a good variety of meat-based meals, or at least anything beyond chicken nuggets! But having some different new ways of serving meat can be key to getting them interested in it again.

APPLE AND CARROT CHICKEN BALLS

| Serves: 4 (makes 20 balls) | Prep time: 10 minutes | Cook time: 20–25 minutes |

Some days my kids just want easy finger food for dinner. These apple and carrot chicken balls are perfect to serve with a few raw vegetables and some dipping sauce on the side. Simple food but still super-healthy.

Ingredients

½ tbsp olive or vegetable oil

1 small onion, finely diced

2 garlic cloves, crushed

1 medium red apple, grated (skin on) and the juice squeezed out

1 medium carrot, grated

450g skinless chicken breasts

1 tsp dried Italian herbs

2 sage leaves, finely chopped

150g cooked quinoa (50g uncooked)

salt and pepper, to taste

lettuce leaves, carrots, cucumber and peppers, to serve

Method

1. Preheat the oven to 200°C/180°C Fan/Gas Mark 6 and line 2 baking trays with baking parchment.

2. Heat the oil in a frying pan over a medium heat, add the onion and fry for 2-3 minutes until soft, then add the garlic, grated apple and grated carrot and cook for a further 3 minutes. Remove from the heat.

3. Put the chicken breasts in a food processor and pulse until they have broken down into a mince.

4. Add the vegetables from the frying pan, along with the dried herbs, chopped sage and a little salt and pepper. Pulse again just enough to combine all the ingredients.

5. Transfer the mixture to a bowl, add the cooked quinoa and mix with a spoon.

6. Using your hands, form the mixture into about 20 balls and place them on the lined baking trays.

7. Bake in the oven for 15-20 minutes, or until the balls are cooked through.

8. Serve in lettuce leaves with a dip. They taste delicious with Sweet Chilli Sauce (see page 187) and sliced raw vegetables such as carrots, cucumber and peppers.

9. The cooked balls can be frozen for up to 3 months. Defrost overnight in the fridge and reheat in the microwave or oven.

PIRI PIRI SPATCHCOCK CHICKEN

| Serves: 6 | Prep time: 5–10 minutes | Cook time: 45–50 minutes |

If you love roast chicken but don't always have time to cook it, then this is the recipe for you. By removing the backbone and flattening the chicken out (known as spatchcocking), you can cut the standard cooking time in half.

Ingredients

1 medium chicken (about 1.75kg)

1 tbsp olive oil

1 tbsp honey

1 tbsp piri piri seasoning

1 tsp smoked paprika

Method

1. Preheat the oven to 220°C/200°C Fan/Gas Mark 7 and line a large baking tray with foil.

2. Place the chicken breast-side down on the tray with the legs closest to you. Using sturdy kitchen scissors, cut either side of the backbone that runs down the centre of the chicken and remove it. Turn the chicken over and flatten it down as much as possible: using your hands, press firmly on the breastbone until it cracks. You should now be able to flatten the chicken out even more. Using a sharp knife, make a few incisions in the leg meat on the chicken. If you like, secure the chicken with two metal skewers by inserting them in a crisscross shape through the chicken.

3. Mix the oil, honey, piri piri seasoning and smoked paprika in a bowl then rub the sauce all over the chicken.

4. Roast in the oven for 45–50 minutes until the chicken is cooked and the juices run clear when you pierce the thickest part of the chicken with a knife.

5. Serve the chicken immediately, with vegetables or salad, and plain rice or Savoury Veggie Rice (see page 117).

MEAL PLAN

CHICKEN AND AUBERGINE KATSU

| Serves: 4 | Prep time: 15 minutes | Cook time: 35 minutes |

This classic Japanese dish may seem tricky to prepare but it's perfect for relaxed weekends when you have more time to devote to making dinner. The key is to get ready first, with your ingredients prepared in bowls. The end result is worth the little bit of effort!

Ingredients

200g long grain or basmati rice

For the curry sauce

½ tbsp vegetable or sunflower oil

1 medium onion, roughly chopped

1 apple, peeled, cored and roughly chopped

1 garlic clove, crushed

1 tbsp mild curry powder

1 tbsp plain flour

300ml vegetable stock

½ tbsp soy sauce

For the katsu

2 skinless chicken breasts

25g plain flour

2 eggs

100g panko breadcrumbs

1 medium aubergine, cut into 1cm-thick slices

3 tbsp vegetable or sunflower oil

Method

1. First, make the curry sauce. Heat the oil in a small saucepan over a medium heat, add the onion and fry for about 2 minutes until it starts to soften, then add the apple and garlic and fry for a further 2 minutes. Add the curry powder and flour and stir for about a minute.

2. Add the vegetable stock and soy sauce, bring to the boil, then reduce the heat and simmer for 10 minutes, or until the sauce has thickened.

3. Remove from the heat and blitz the sauce with a hand-held blender or in a stand blender until smooth. Set aside and cover to keep warm.

4. Cook the rice in another saucepan accordingly to the packet instructions.

5. Place the chicken breasts next to each other between two pieces of cling film and lay them on a chopping board. Use a rolling pin to bash the breasts down until they are about half their original thickness.

6. Get an assembly line ready by putting the flour in a large bowl, cracking the eggs into another large bowl and whisking them with a fork, and putting the panko breadcrumbs into a third bowl. Finally, put a large empty plate or tray at the end of the assembly line on which to place the coated chicken and aubergine.

7. Starting with the aubergine, coat each slice in some flour, dip in the beaten egg then cover with breadcrumbs. Place on the plate. Repeat with the rest of the aubergine slices then do the same with the flattened chicken breasts.

8. Once all the meat and veg has been coated, heat the oil in a large frying pan over a medium heat.

9. Fry the coated aubergine in batches for about 2 minutes on either side, remove and leave to drain on kitchen paper, then fry the coated chicken for about 5 minutes on either side until crispy on the outside and cooked through.

10. Drain on kitchen paper then slice the chicken into strips.

11. Pour the curry sauce into a jug or bowl and serve in the middle of the table with a big bowl of rice and a plate full of chicken and aubergine.

SWEET AND SOUR CHICKEN

| Serves: 4 | Prep time: 5 minutes | Cook time: 35 minutes |

Making this takeaway favourite at home is super-easy and it's a great way to introduce kids to slightly more exotic flavours.

Ingredients

400g skinless chicken breasts, diced

2 tbsp cornflour

1 tbsp sesame oil

2 sweet peppers, halved, deseeded and roughly chopped

1 onion, chopped

130g pineapple chunks (fresh or tinned)

For the sweet and sour sauce
4 tbsp pineapple juice

2 tbsp rice wine vinegar

2 tbsp soy sauce

1 tbsp tomato purée

1 tbsp honey

1 garlic clove, crushed

pinch of salt and pepper

Method

1. Put the diced chicken and cornflour into a large bowl and mix well until all the chicken is coated.

2. Put the sauce ingredients in a mug or jug and mix well.

3. Heat the oil in a large frying pan or wok over a medium high heat, add the coated chicken and fry for about 10 minutes until the chicken is golden brown, crispy and cooked through.

4. Add the peppers and onion and fry for a further 2–3 minutes, then add the pineapple chunks and the sauce. Cook for 1–2 minutes until the sauce thickens.

5. Serve immediately with rice.

6. This dish will keep covered in the fridge for up to 2 days.

GREEK CHICKEN TRAYBAKE

| Serves: 4 | Prep time: 5 minutes | Cook time: 35–40 minutes |

Mid-week I love nothing more than a one-pot meal, and this recipe is so easy:
all the main ingredients are cooked together in one dish in the oven
and the dip ingredients just need a quick mix!

Ingredients

For the traybake

8 chicken thighs

3 peppers (a combination of colours), halved, deseeded and roughly chopped

1 red onion, cut into wedges

2 garlic cloves, roughly chopped

100g cherry tomatoes, halved

50g pitted black olives

1 tbsp olive oil

1 tbsp honey

juice of ½ lemon

1 tsp dried oregano

½ tsp smoked paprika

50g feta cheese

For the tzatziki dip

150g plain Greek yoghurt

¼ cucumber, finely diced

1 garlic clove, crushed

½ tsp mint sauce

salt and pepper, to taste

Method

1. Preheat the oven to 200°C/180°C Fan/Gas Mark 6. Put the chicken thighs, peppers, onion, garlic, cherry tomatoes and olives in a large baking dish and mix.

2. Put the olive oil, honey, lemon juice, oregano and smoked paprika in a jug or mug and whisk together with a fork. Pour this mixture over the chicken and vegetables and mix thoroughly until everything is well coated.

3. Bake in the oven for 35–40 minutes until the chicken thighs are cooked through and the skin is crisp and brown.

4. Remove from the oven and crumble the feta cheese over the top.

5. To make the dip, combine the yoghurt, cucumber, garlic and mint sauce in a bowl. Season to taste with salt and pepper.

6. Serve the chicken traybake and tzatziki dip with toasted pitta bread.

CHICKEN DIPPERS WITH HONEY MUSTARD MAYO

  GF DF KM

| Serves: 4 | Prep time: 10 minutes | Cook time: 7 minutes |

These chicken dippers are my healthier take on nuggets. I use ground almonds to coat the chicken instead of breadcrumbs, which makes a fine-textured but really tasty coating.

Ingredients

For the chicken dippers

400g chicken mini fillets or skinless chicken breasts, cut into strips

2 eggs

70g ground almonds

large pinch of ground cumin

salt and pepper, to taste

2 tbsp olive or vegetable oil

For the honey mustard mayo

75g mayonnaise (see page 185 for my homemade mayo)

1 tsp honey

½ tsp Dijon mustard

Method

1. Get an assembly line ready by placing the chicken strips on a plate, cracking the eggs into a large bowl and whisking them with a fork and combining the ground almonds and cumin with a little salt and pepper in another bowl. Finally, put an empty plate at the end of the assembly line on which to place the coated chicken.

2. Dip a chicken strip in the egg, then coat it in the almond mixture and place it on the empty plate. Repeat with the remaining chicken strips.

3. Heat the oil in a large frying pan over a medium heat and, when the oil is very hot, add the coated chicken strips. Fry for about 4 minutes then turn them over and cook for a further 3 minutes until the chicken is crispy and brown on the outside and cooked through.

4. To make the honey mustard mayo, combine all the ingredients in a small bowl.

5. Serve the chicken dippers with the mayo for dipping and some Crispy Sweet Potato Fries (see page 120) or Easy Potato Wedges (see page 120).

MEAL PLAN

BEEF AND PEARL BARLEY CASSEROLE

| Serves: 4 | Prep time: 10 minutes | Cook time: 1 hour 40 minutes |

This casserole is the ultimate cold-weather comfort food. It takes a bit of time
to cook but it's worth every minute of the wait. It's also ideal for cooking
in bulk so you can freeze half for another day.

Ingredients

1 tbsp olive or vegetable oil

500g diced stewing beef

1 large carrot, finely chopped

1 medium parsnip, finely chopped

300g butternut squash or swede,
   peeled and chopped

150g whole button mushrooms

100g silverskin onions (from a jar)

2 garlic cloves, crushed

1 litre beef stock, plus extra
   if needed

100ml red wine (optional)

2 tbsp tomato purée

4 sprigs fresh thyme

100g pearl barley

crusty bread, to serve

Method

1. Heat the oil in a large casserole dish or wide saucepan
   over a medium heat. Add the diced beef and fry for
   about 5 minutes until the meat has browned, then
   add the carrot, parsnip, squash or swede, mushrooms,
   silverskin onions and garlic and fry for a further
   3 minutes.

2. Add about 700ml of the beef stock, red wine, if using,
   tomato purée and thyme, bring to the boil, then reduce
   the heat and simmer uncovered for 1 hour.

3. Check the casserole regularly and add more beef stock
   if needed.

4. After 1 hour, add the pearl barley and cook for a further
   30 minutes.

5. Serve with chunks of crusty bread. The casserole, once
   cool, can be stored in an airtight container in the fridge
   for up to 2 days, or in the freezer for up to 3 months.

LOADED NACHOS

| Serves: 4 | Prep time: 10 minutes | Cook time: 17 minutes |

These loaded nachos are a regular Saturday night treat in my house. My kids love how fun they are and it's nice for us all to share food out of one big dish.

Ingredients

3 large tortilla wraps

1 tbsp olive or vegetable oil

500g lean minced beef

1 tsp ground cumin

1 tsp smoked paprika

1 tsp ground coriander

½ tsp mild chilli powder

½ tsp garlic powder

150ml beef stock

50g grated Cheddar cheese

1 red pepper, halved, deseeded and finely diced

1 yellow pepper, halved, deseeded and finely diced

10 cherry tomatoes, quartered

2 spring onions, finely diced

sour cream, chopped fresh coriander and lime wedges, to serve

Method

1. Preheat the oven to 200°C/180°C Fan/Gas Mark 6 and line 2 baking trays with baking parchment or foil.

2. Stack the tortilla wraps on top of each other and cut the stack into 8 triangles, as if you were cutting a pizza, to make 24 triangles in total.

3. Brush both sides of the tortilla chips with a little oil and place them on the baking trays (if there's not enough room on the trays you may have to bake them in batches).

4. Bake the chips in the oven for 5–6 minutes, turning them over halfway through. You want them just turning crispy but not too brown.

5. Meanwhile, heat the remaining oil in a frying pan over a medium heat, add the mince and fry for 4–5 minutes until browned. Add the spices and garlic powder and mix well. Add the beef stock and simmer for 10 minutes until the stock has reduced right down.

6. Once the tortilla chips are all baked, put them into a baking dish (I use a 27 x 22cm dish). Add the cooked mince on top then scatter over the toppings – grated cheese, peppers, cherry tomatoes and spring onions.

7. Bake in the oven for 5 minutes.

8. Remove from the oven and serve the loaded nachos in the dish with sour cream, fresh coriander and lime wedges on the side.

TOAD IN THE HOLE

GF KM

| Serves: 4 | Prep time: 5 minutes | Cook time: 40 minutes |

This old favourite has been making a bit of a comeback recently. Use really good-quality, flavour-packed sausages and serve with your choice of veggies.

Ingredients

50ml sunflower oil

6 good-quality sausages

150g plain flour

3 eggs

220ml whole milk

½ tsp Dijon mustard

pinch of pepper

200g green vegetables (broccoli, beans, asparagus, etc.), cooked

Method

1. Preheat the oven to 220°C/200°C Fan/Gas Mark 7.

2. Put the oil and the sausages in a baking dish (I use a 27 x 22cm dish) and cook the sausages in the oven for 10 minutes, turning them once, just to brown them.

3. In a large jug whisk together the flour, eggs and milk. Add the mustard and pepper and whisk again.

4. Remove the baking dish from the oven and pour the batter on top of the sausages. Return the dish to the oven for a further 30 minutes.

5. Meanwhile, boil or steam the green vegetables.

6. When the toad in the hole is cooked, remove the dish from the oven and serve immediately with the cooked green vegetables.

FISH

If your family's love of fish doesn't go beyond fish fingers then don't worry,
you're not alone. My children really struggle with fish but by getting
a bit creative with how I serve it, they will now at least try
a few bites! The key is to serve it in a way that's already
familiar to them – with their favourite pasta,
topped with pesto and cheese or
made to look like meatballs.

TUNA MEATBALLS

| Serves: 4 | Prep time: 10 minutes | Cook time: 15 minutes |

Tuna is a brilliant purse-friendly fish and when it's made into 'meatballs' it makes a great recipe to try if your kids are not fish fans. Cooking the tuna softens the flavour and serving it up with spaghetti makes this dish more recognisable to picky eaters.

Ingredients

1 small carrot, grated

1 small courgette, grated

2 x 160g tins tuna in water or brine, drained

50g breadcrumbs

1 egg

1 garlic clove, crushed

1 spring onion, finely diced

1 tsp lemon juice

300g dried spaghetti

2 tbsp olive or vegetable oil

400g tin chopped tomatoes

2 tbsp tomato purée

½ tsp dried oregano

salt and pepper, to taste

Method

1. Squeeze out as much of the juice from the grated carrot and courgette as possible then put the grated vegetables in a bowl and add the drained tuna, breadcrumbs, egg, garlic, spring onion and lemon juice. Season with a little salt and pepper. Form the mixture into 12 balls and set them aside.

2. Cook the spaghetti in a large pan of boiling water according to the packet instructions.

3. Heat the oil in a large frying pan over a medium heat, add the tuna meatballs and fry for 5-6 minutes until browned all over. Once cooked, transfer the meatballs to a bowl.

4. Add the chopped tomatoes, tomato purée and dried oregano to the frying pan and cook for about 5 minutes until the sauce has thickened.

5. Drain the spaghetti and mix it in with the tomato sauce. You might want to retain a little of the pasta water to help loosen the sauce if it seems a bit too thick.

6. Serve the spaghetti immediately, with the tuna meatballs on top.

PESTO SALMON BAKE WITH COUSCOUS

GF   KM

| Serves: 4 | Prep time: 5 minutes | Cook time: 20 minutes |

This is a really quick and simple family meal that's perfect for busy weekdays.
You can swap the salmon for other fish, depending on your preferences.

Ingredients

4 salmon fillets (skin on or skinless)

100g pesto (see page 78 for
my Popeye's Protein Pesto)

150g cherry tomatoes

1 green pepper, halved, deseeded
and roughly chopped

1 yellow pepper, halved, deseeded
and roughly chopped

15g grated Parmesan cheese

150g frozen mixed chopped
vegetables

750ml hot vegetable stock

150g couscous

Method

1. Preheat the oven to 200°C/180°C Fan/Gas Mark 6.

2. Place the salmon fillets in a large baking dish and
spread the pesto on top. Add the cherry tomatoes and
peppers to the dish and bake in the oven for 10 minutes.

3. After 10 minutes, remove the baking dish and sprinkle
the Parmesan on top of the salmon. Return to the oven
for a further 10 minutes.

4. Put the frozen vegetables and stock into a large jug and
cook in the microwave for 1–2 minutes until the veggies
are hot.

5. Put the couscous in a heatproof bowl and pour in the
veggies and stock, adding just enough stock to cover
the couscous. Put a plate on top of the bowl and leave
for 5–10 minutes until the stock has been absorbed.

6. Remove the salmon and vegetables from the oven and
serve alongside the couscous.

MEAL PLAN

ONE-POT SALMON LINGUINE

 GF DF

| Serves: 4 | Prep time: 2 minutes | Cook time: 10 minutes |

I'm a big fan of one-pot pasta meals and this salmon version doesn't disappoint.
It's so quick and easy to make and is a great way of making
a small amount of salmon go far.

Ingredients

250g skinless salmon fillet, cut into
large chunks

300g linguine, strands broken in half

400g tin coconut milk

500ml hot vegetable stock

1 red pepper, halved, deseeded
and diced

75g baby corn, halved

50g mangetout

1 garlic clove, crushed

1 shallot, diced

1 tsp medium curry powder

Method

1. Put all the ingredients in a large saucepan or shallow
casserole dish and bring to the boil over a medium heat.

2. Reduce the heat and simmer for 8–10 minutes until the
spaghetti and salmon are cooked and all the stock has
been absorbed, stirring regularly.

3. Serve immediately.

BURGERS

Nothing beats a delicious juicy burger for dinner and making your own at home doesn't have to be hard work at all. My tried-and-tested beef, chicken and veggie burgers are all easy to make and packed with nutritional fresh ingredients.

LENTIL VEGGIE BURGER

| Serves: 4 | Prep time: 10 minutes | Cook time: 6 minutes |

If you have lots of veg left over after a big Sunday roast, don't throw it away. Mix it with some tinned lentils to make these really tasty veggie burgers the following day.

Ingredients

250g cooked vegetables (such as carrots, cauliflower, broccoli, potato and squash)

100g drained tinned lentils

½ red onion, finely diced

1 garlic clove, crushed

50g breadcrumbs

75g grated Cheddar cheese

1 egg

½ tsp dried Italian herbs

½ tsp smoked paprika

2 tbsp plain flour

1 tbsp olive or vegetable oil

salt and pepper, to taste

burger buns, lettuce, and tomato and cucumber slices, to serve

Method

1. Mash the cooked vegetables as much as you can and place them in a large bowl with the lentils, red onion, garlic, breadcrumbs, grated cheese, egg, herbs and smoked paprika. Mix until well combined. Season to taste with salt and pepper.

2. Shape the mixture into 4 burgers.

3. Spread the flour out on a large plate then coat each burger in the flour.

4. Place the burgers on a plate in the freezer for 20 minutes. This is an important step as these burgers are very soft and are prone to falling apart when cooked: the freezing time will help hold them together.

5. Heat the oil in a frying pan over a medium heat and fry the burgers for about 3 minutes on each side until they are fully warmed through.

6. Remove from the heat and serve in burger buns with lettuce, tomato and cucumber.

TROPICAL CHICKEN BURGER

| Serves: 4 | Prep time: 15 minutes | Cook time: 14 minutes |

Even the most chicken-adverse children (my daughter included) are sure
to enjoy these tasty burgers packed with sweet veggies and fruit.

Ingredients

400g skinless chicken breasts

½ mango, finely chopped

½ red pepper, finely chopped

1 garlic clove, crushed

1 spring onion, finely chopped

50g drained tinned sweetcorn
(or defrosted frozen sweetcorn)

1 egg

juice of ½ lime

2 tbsp plain flour

1 tbsp olive or vegetable oil

4 rings of tinned pineapple

salt and pepper, to taste

burger buns, lettuce or spinach,
and tomato and cucumber slices,
to serve

Method

1. Put the chicken into a food processor and blitz until it has broken down, almost to a mince consistency. Transfer the minced chicken to a large bowl. Add the mango, red pepper, garlic, spring onion, sweetcorn, egg and lime juice and mix well. Season with a little salt and pepper.

2. Shape the mixture into 4 large burgers.

3. Spread the flour out on a large plate then coat each burger in the flour.

4. If you have time, put the burgers in the fridge for up to 1 hour as this helps to firm them up.

5. Heat the oil in a frying pan or griddle pan over a medium heat and fry the burgers for about 6 minutes on each side until they are fully cooked through.

6. Remove the burgers from the pan and fry the pineapple rings for 1 minute on each side.

7. Serve the chicken burgers in burger buns (toast them on a griddle pan first, if you like) with a pineapple ring, lettuce or spinach, tomato and cucumber.

MELTY MOZZARELLA BEEF BURGER

 GF KM

| Serves: 4 | Prep time: 15 minutes | Cook time: 12 minutes |

Everyone loves a tasty homemade burger. I've put a spin on the classic beef
burger by adding a melty mozzarella surprise in the middle!

Ingredients

1 shallot, finely diced

1 garlic clove, crushed

500g minced beef

1 egg

1 tsp dried oregano

75g mozzarella cheese

2 tbsp plain flour

1 tbsp olive or sunflower oil

salt and pepper, to taste

burger buns, lettuce, and tomato
and cucumber slices, to serve

Method

1. Combine the shallot, garlic, minced beef, egg and dried
   oregano in a bowl. Season with a little salt and pepper.

2. Shape the mixture roughly into 4 large burgers.

3. Using your thumb, create a hole in the middle of each
   burger and push in a quarter of the mozzarella. Shape
   the meat around the cheese so that it's hidden inside
   the burger.

4. Spread the flour out on a large plate, then coat each
   burger in the flour.

5. If you have time, put the burgers in the fridge for
   up to 1 hour as this helps to firm them up.

6. Heat the oil in a frying pan over a medium heat and fry
   the burgers for about 6 minutes on each side until they
   are fully cooked through.

7. Remove from the heat and serve in burger buns with
   lettuce, tomato and cucumber.

VEGGIE SIDES

Hiding veggies in meals is a brilliant way to pack some nutrition into your family's diet if they're reluctant veg eaters, but it's also great to celebrate vegetables for what they are – fresh, colourful, delicious and nutritious!
These side dishes are ideal for serving up alongside lunch or dinner and to make veggies at the dinner table the norm.

SALAD CUPS

| Serves: 4 | Prep time: 5 minutes | Cook time: 7–8 minutes |

No more boring salads! Liven up the humble salad by making these fun tortilla cups.
Add lettuce, tomatoes, peppers and carrots or any of your favourite ingredients.

Ingredients

1 large tortilla wrap

4 lettuce leaves, chopped

4 cherry tomatoes, chopped

½ yellow pepper, chopped

½ carrot, grated

Method

1. Preheat the oven to 200°C/180°C Fan/Gas Mark 6.

2. Use a 9cm or 10cm pastry cutter to cut out 4 circles from the tortilla wrap. Press each of the tortilla circles into a hole in a muffin tray and bake for 7–8 minutes until crisp.

3. Remove from the oven and set them aside to cool.

4. Meanwhile, get the salad fillings ready and, once the tortilla cups are cooled, fill them with the salad. Serve immediately.

SAVOURY VEGGIE RICE

| Serves: 4 | Prep time: 5 minutes | Cook time: 20 minutes |

This homemade savoury veggie rice makes a delicious and filling side dish to any meal.
It can also be cooled and served up as a rice salad the following day.

Ingredients

200g easy-cook white rice

650ml hot vegetable stock

1 tsp medium curry powder

½ tsp turmeric

200g frozen mixed chopped vegetables

1 red pepper, halved, deseeded and finely diced

Method

1. Put the rice and vegetable stock into a large saucepan, place over a medium heat and bring to the boil, then reduce the heat and stir in the curry powder and turmeric. Simmer for 15 minutes, or until the rice is cooked and the stock has been absorbed.

2. Add the frozen vegetables and red pepper and cook for a further 3-4 minutes until the vegetables are warmed through.

3. Serve immediately or cool and store in an airtight container in the fridge for up to 3 days.

CORN ON THE COB POPS

| Serves: 4 | Prep time: 2 minutes | Cook time: 6 minutes |

Kids love corn but make it even more fun by serving cobs on a stick spread with some garlic butter. Perfect to serve as a side dish or even as a snack.

Ingredients

4 mini corn on the cob
(fresh or frozen)

2 tbsp butter, softened

1 garlic clove, crushed

4 ice lolly sticks

Method

1. Cook the mini corn on the cob in a saucepan of boiling water for 6–8 minutes, or until the corn is soft and cooked.

2. Make the garlic butter by mixing the butter and garlic together in a small bowl.

3. Drain the corn and let it cool slightly before inserting the lolly sticks into the centre of each cob.

4. Serve the corn on the cob immediately with the garlic butter.

EASY POTATO WEDGES

| Serves: 4 | Prep time: 6 minutes | Cook time: 15–17 minutes |

Leaving the skins on the potatoes means these wedges are super-easy to make, and they are more nutritious, too.

Ingredients

600g baby new potatoes, washed (but skins left on) and quartered (or just halved, if very small)

1 tbsp olive oil

½ tsp dried Italian herbs

Method

1. Preheat the oven to 220°C/200°C Fan/Gas Mark 7 and line a baking tray with baking parchment.

2. Put the potato wedges into a large bowl with the oil and herbs, toss to coat, then transfer to the lined tray.

3. Roast in the oven for 15–17 minutes until cooked through and crispy. Serve immediately.

CRISPY SWEET POTATO FRIES

| Serves: 4 | Prep time: 5 minutes | Cook time: 15–20 minutes |

A light coating of cornflour helps to add some crispiness to these tasty homemade sweet potato fries.

Ingredients

700g sweet potatoes, washed (but skins left on) and cut into thin fries

1 tbsp cornflour

½ tsp dried Italian herbs

¼ tsp smoked paprika

1 tbsp olive oil

salt and pepper, to taste

Method

1. Preheat the oven to 240°C/220°C Fan/Gas Mark 9 and line a baking tray with baking parchment.

2. Put the sweet potato fries into a large bowl with the cornflour. Mix with your hands to coat the sweet potato fries in the cornflour, then shake off any excess.

3. Add the herbs, smoked paprika, oil and a little salt and pepper, then transfer the fries to the lined tray.

4. Roast in the oven for 15–20 minutes, turning the fries halfway through. Remove from the oven and serve immediately.

CREAMY CAULIFLOWER MASHED POTATO

| Serves: 4 | Prep time: 5 minutes | Cook time: 10–12 minutes |

Boost the nutritional value of your mash by adding cauliflower. It's just as delicious as regular mashed potato, and super-creamy, too.

Ingredients

450g white potatoes, peeled and cut into small chunks

250g cauliflower, cut into small florets

50ml milk

30g butter

salt and pepper, to taste

Method

1. Put the potato and cauliflower into a saucepan and cover with boiling water. Cook over a medium heat for 10–12 minutes until the potato and cauliflower are soft.

2. Drain well then transfer the vegetables to a food processor. Add the milk and butter and blitz until smooth. Season to taste with salt and pepper.

3. Serve immediately or leave to cool and store in an airtight container in the fridge for up to 3 days.

RAINBOW VEGGIE KEBABS

| Serves: 4 | Prep time: 6 minutes | Cook time: 6 minutes |

Bright, fun and all the colours of the rainbow, these veggie kebabs make a really healthy addition to any meal and can be cooked outside on the barbecue in the summer. You will need 4 long skewers.

Ingredients

4 baby corn, halved

1 red pepper, halved, deseeded and roughly chopped

1 green pepper, halved, deseeded and roughly chopped

1 courgette, roughly chopped

1 red onion, roughly chopped

8 button mushrooms

8 cherry tomatoes

1 tbsp olive oil

pinch of dried Italian herbs

Method

1. If you are using wooden skewers soak them in water for about 10 minutes before using, to stop them from burning. Preheat the grill.

2. Push all the vegetables onto the skewers, alternating them on each skewer. Place the skewers on a grill tray.

3. Mix the oil and herbs in a small bowl and brush the oil over the skewered veggies with a pastry brush.

4. Grill for 3-4 minutes then turn and brush the other side of each skewer with oil and grill for a further 3-4 minutes. Serve immediately.

SNACKS

BATCH-MADE

My kids love to snack. They are still young, and growing fast, so snacking plays an important role in their daily calorie and nutritional intake. For me, the key to healthier snacking is having a selection of pre-made snacks in the fridge or cupboard, ready to whip out at a moment's notice!

All of these snacks can be made in bulk and kept for several days. If weekdays are hectic for you then try making just one or two of them at the weekend, ready for the week ahead.

FRUITY FLAPJACKS

| Makes: 12 flapjacks | Prep time: 5 minutes | Cook time: 22 minutes |

These oaty nut-free flapjacks are packed with fruity flavours.
Brilliant for afternoon snacks or to add to lunchboxes.

Ingredients

120 unsalted butter, plus extra
   for greasing

60g honey

juice of 1 clementine or 2 tbsp
   orange juice

150g rolled oats

40g desiccated coconut

50g plain flour

100g dried fruit (I use raisins,
   chopped apricots and cranberries)

25g mixed seeds (pumpkin,
   sunflower and linseeds)

Method

1. Preheat the oven to 200°C/180°C Fan/Gas Mark 6.
   Grease and line a baking dish or baking tin with baking
   parchment (I use a 20cm square dish).

2. Melt the butter in a small saucepan or in a jug in the
   microwave and mix in the honey and clementine
   or orange juice.

3. Put the oats, coconut, flour, dried fruit and seeds in a
   large bowl and mix well. Pour the butter mixture into
   the bowl and give everything a good stir.

4. Transfer the mixture to the lined dish and press it down
   firmly with the back of a spoon. I also like to take a piece
   of baking parchment and use it to press down firmly
   with my hands, making the mixture as compact as possible.

5. Bake in the oven for 20 minutes, or until the edges of the
   flapjack start to turn golden brown.

6. Remove from the oven and leave to cool a little then
   transfer the dish to the fridge for 1 hour to cool
   completely and harden. This stops the bars falling
   apart once cut.

7. Remove from the fridge and lift the baking parchment
   out of the dish. Cut the flapjack into 12 small squares.

8. These flapjacks will keep in the fridge for up to 4 days.

ENERGY BITES 4 WAYS

| Each recipe makes 12 bites | Prep time: 5 minutes |

These energy bites are packed with nutritious and filling ingredients, making them the perfect afternoon snack for peckish kids. They're great for making in bulk and keeping in the fridge, where they will keep for up to 5 days in an airtight container.

MANGO, LIME AND COCONUT ENERGY BITES

Ingredients

100g rolled oats

120g smooth peanut butter

2 tbsp honey

2 tbsp ground flaxseed

2 tbsp desiccated coconut

25g dried mango, finely chopped

grated zest and juice of 1 lime

½ tsp vanilla extract

Method

1. Put all the ingredients in a large bowl and mix until well combined.

2. Roll the mixture into 12 bite-sized balls and place them on a small plate.

3. Put into the fridge for 1 hour to allow them to firm up.

CHOCOLATE CHIP ENERGY BITES

Ingredients

100g rolled oats

120g smooth peanut butter

2 tbsp honey

2 tbsp ground flaxseed

2 tbsp desiccated coconut

½ tsp vanilla extract

50g dark or milk chocolate chips

Method

1. Put all the ingredients, except the chocolate chips, into a large bowl and mix until well combined.

2. Fold in the chocolate chips.

3. Roll the mixture into 12 bite-sized balls and place them on a small plate.

4. Put into the fridge for 1 hour to allow them to firm up.

Recipe continues overleaf

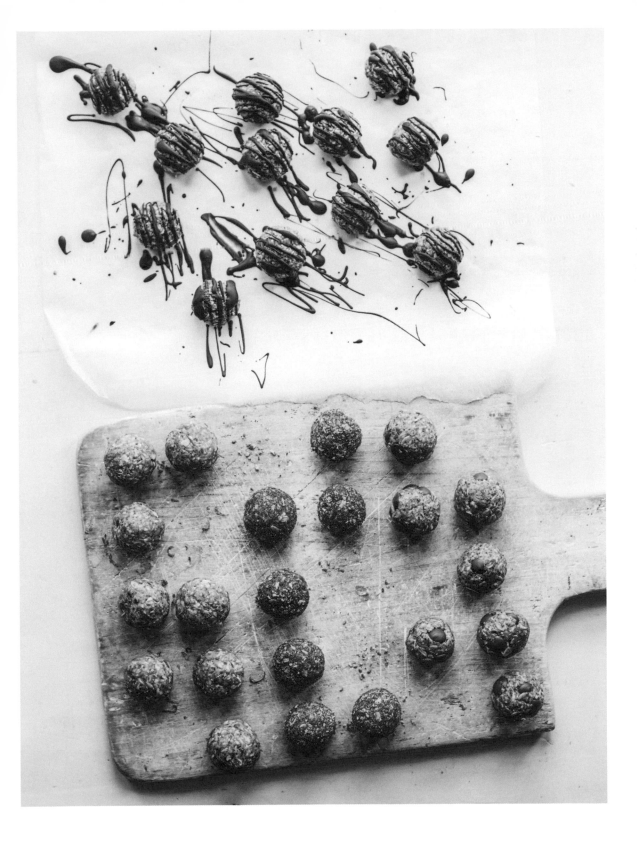

RASPBERRY COCONUT ENERGY BITES

Ingredients

100g rolled oats

120g smooth peanut butter

2 tbsp honey

2 tbsp ground flaxseed

2 tbsp desiccated coconut

½ tsp vanilla extract

2 tbsp freeze-dried raspberries,
plus 2 tbsp for coating

2 tbsp shredded coconut,
for coating

Method

1. Put all the ingredients into a large bowl and mix until well combined.

2. Roll the mixture into 12 bite-sized balls and place them on a small plate.

3. Put the coating ingredients into a food processor and blitz until fine and powder-like, then transfer to a plate.

4. Roll the energy bites in the blitzed raspberries and coconut, transfer to a clean plate and put them into the fridge for 1 hour to allow them to firm up.

CHOCOLATE ORANGE ENERGY BITES

Ingredients

100g rolled oats

120g smooth peanut butter

2 tbsp honey

2 tbsp ground flaxseed

2 tbsp desiccated coconut

1 tbsp orange juice

grated zest of ½ orange

½ tsp vanilla extract

2 squares of dark chocolate

Method

1. Put all the ingredients, except the chocolate, into a large bowl and mix until well combined.

2. Roll the mixture into 12 bite-sized balls and place them on a small plate.

3. Put into the fridge for 1 hour to allow them to firm up.

4. Melt the chocolate and drizzle it over the energy bites. Put them back in the fridge for a further 10 minutes.

CHOCOLATE CHIP GRANOLA BARS

  KM

| Makes: 8 large or 16 small bars | Prep time: 10 minutes | Cook time: 30 minutes |

Crispy, crunchy and chewy, these no-bake chocolate chip granola bars
are the perfect mid-afternoon snack for hungry kids.

Ingredients

125g rolled oats

25g puffed rice cereal

100g smooth peanut butter

100g honey

50g coconut oil or unsalted butter

25g milk or dark chocolate chips

Method

1. Line a 20cm square baking dish or tin with baking parchment.

2. Combine the oats and puffed rice cereal in a large bowl.

3. Put the peanut butter, honey and coconut oil or butter into a saucepan and heat gently until melted.

4. Pour this mixture over the oats and rice cereal and mix well.

5. Allow the mixture to cool (you can put it in the fridge) then add the chocolate chips and mix again.

6. Transfer the mixture to the lined dish and use the back of a spoon to press it down well. I also like to use a piece of baking parchment to press down firmly with my hands and make the mixture as compact as possible.

7. Place the dish in the freezer for 30 minutes, then remove and cut into 8 large or 16 small bars.

8. These granola bars will keep in the fridge for up to 4 days.

CRANBERRY AND COCONUT COOKIES

| Makes: 10 cookies | Prep time: 10 minutes | Cook time: 15 minutes |

Hearty cookies made with oats, wholemeal flour and less sugar than shop-bought versions. These cookies make the perfect after-school snack for hungry kids.

Ingredients

50g dried cranberries

120g unsalted butter, softened

40g soft light brown sugar

½ tsp vanilla extract

100g wholewheat flour

100g rolled oats

20g desiccated coconut

¼ tsp bicarbonate of soda

Method

1. Preheat the oven to 180°C/160°C Fan/Gas Mark 4 and line 2 baking trays with baking parchment.

2. Put the dried cranberries into a small heatproof bowl and cover with hot water. Leave for a few minutes to soak.

3. Meanwhile, put the butter, sugar and vanilla extract into a large bowl and beat together to combine. Add the flour, oats, coconut and bicarbonate of soda and mix with a spoon, then drain the cranberries and add them to the bowl, mixing one final time.

4. Divide the mixture into 10 equal-sized balls and place on the lined baking trays.

5. Use a spoon to push the balls down and shape them into a cookie shape. Bake in the oven for 15 minutes.

6. Remove from the oven and leave the cookies to cool on the baking tray for 5 minutes (they will still be quite soft) before transferring them to a wire rack to cool completely.

7. The cookies will keep in an airtight container at room temperature for up to 3 days.

OATY CHOCOLATE BISCUITS

GF   BC   KM

| Makes: 12 biscuits | Prep time: 10 minutes | Cook time: 12–14 minutes |

These homemade chocolate oat biscuits are my healthier take on the packet version. Made with rolled oats and wholemeal flour they contain more fibre and less sugar, too.

Ingredients

100g rolled oats

100g wholemeal flour

½ tsp baking powder

¼ tsp bicarbonate of soda

75g unsalted butter or coconut oil, melted

50g honey

½ tsp vanilla extract

50g milk or dark chocolate, broken into pieces

Method

1. Preheat the oven to 180°C/160°C Fan/Gas Mark 4 and line 2 baking trays with baking parchment.

2. Combine the oats, flour, baking powder and bicarbonate of soda in a large bowl.

3. In a second bowl mix together the melted butter or coconut oil, honey and vanilla extract.

4. Add the wet ingredients to the dry ingredients and mix well with a spoon.

5. Take a heaped tablespoon of the mixture, place it on the lined baking tray and use your hands to mould it into a round biscuit shape. You should be able to make 12 biscuits from the mixture.

6. Bake in the oven for 12-14 minutes until the biscuits are starting to brown around the edges.

7. Remove from the oven and leave the biscuits to cool on the baking tray for 5 minutes (they will still be quite soft) before transferring them to a wire rack to cool completely.

8. Once cooled, melt the chocolate and spread it on top of the biscuits.

9. The biscuits will keep in an airtight container at room temperature for up to 3 days.

CARROT AND ORANGE GREEK YOGHURT MUFFINS

| Makes: 12 muffins | Prep time: 10 minutes | Cook time: 20–25 minutes |

These tasty muffins are flavoured with carrot and orange and made with Greek yoghurt, making them a super-healthy and filling after-school snack that kids will love.

Ingredients

250g plain flour

1½ tsp baking powder

½ tsp bicarbonate of soda

75g butter or coconut oil, melted

75g honey

1 egg

75g plain Greek yoghurt

juice of ½ orange

1 tsp grated orange zest

1 tsp vanilla extract

100g grated carrot

Method

1. Preheat the oven to 200°C/180°C Fan/Gas Mark 6 and line a muffin tray with 12 silicone or paper muffin cases.

2. Combine the flour, baking powder and bicarbonate of soda in a large bowl.

3. In a large jug mix together the melted butter or coconut oil, honey, egg, Greek yoghurt, orange juice and zest and vanilla extract. Add the grated carrot and mix again.

4. Add the wet ingredients to the dry ingredients and stir just enough so everything is well combined.

5. Use an ice cream scoop or spoon to fill the muffin cases then bake in the oven for 20-25 minutes until a skewer inserted into the middle of a muffin comes out clean.

6. These muffins will keep in an airtight container at room temperature for up to 3 days. They can also be frozen for up to 3 months, then defrosted at room temperature.

CHOCOLATE CHIP PEANUT BUTTER MUFFINS

| Makes: 10 muffins | Prep time: 10 minutes | Cook time: 15–18 minutes |

These tasty oaty muffins are packed full of energy-dense foods,
making them the perfect snack for busy kids.

Ingredients

1 medium ripe banana, peeled
  and mashed

100g apple sauce (see page 186
  for my homemade apple sauce)

80ml milk

75g smooth peanut butter

1 egg

1 tsp vanilla extract

1 tbsp honey

150g rolled oats

2 tbsp ground flaxseed

½ tsp baking powder

¼ tsp bicarbonate of soda

30g milk or dark chocolate chips

20g milk or dark chocolate, melted,
  for topping (optional)

1 tbsp peanuts, crushed, for
  topping (optional)

Method

1. Preheat the oven to 200°C/180°C Fan/Gas Mark 6 and line a muffin tray with 10 muffin cases (I use silicone cases, but you can use paper cases).

2. Combine the mashed banana, apple sauce, milk, peanut butter, egg, vanilla extract and honey in a large bowl and mix with a whisk.

3. Add the oats, ground flaxseed, baking powder and bicarbonate of soda and mix well with a spoon. Finally, fold in the chocolate chips.

4. Use an ice cream scoop or spoon to fill the muffin cases with the mixture, then bake in the oven for 15–18 minutes, or until a skewer inserted into the middle of one of the muffins comes out clean.

5. Remove from the oven and leave to cool for at least 15 minutes. Top with the melted chocolate and crushed peanuts, if using, before serving.

6. The muffins will keep in an airtight container in the fridge for up to 3 days or can be frozen for up to 3 months and defrosted at room temperature.

FROZEN TREATS

Regardless of what the weather is like outside, kids seem to love ice cream and ice lollies all year round. Making your own frozen treats is a lot easier than you think and by using lots of fresh fruit, yoghurt and even plain old bananas, you can also pack in lots of nutritious ingredients, too.

YOGHURT PUDDING POPS

| Serves: 4 | Prep time: 5 minutes | Freezing time: 4–5 hours |

Turn a standard pot of yoghurt into something a little more exciting for kids by making these fun yoghurt pudding pops!

Ingredients

4 flavoured yoghurt pots
(at least 80g each)

4 tbsp granola (see page 23 for my homemade granola)

4 strawberries, hulled and chopped

Method

1. Remove the lids from the yoghurts.

2. Sprinkle the granola onto the yoghurt and add some chopped strawberries.

3. Insert a stick into the middle of the yoghurt and place in the freezer for 3–4 hours.

4. Remove from the freezer and run the yoghurt pot under running cold water to help remove the pudding pop from the pot.

LEFTOVER SMOOTHIE POPS

| Prep time: 5 minutes | Freezing time: 4–5 hours |

Don't throw away that leftover smoothie. Instead, turn it into a delicious frozen-smoothie popsicle that the kids can enjoy another day.

Ingredients

any leftover smoothie

Method

1. Pour your leftover smoothie into mini popsicle bags or popsicle moulds.

2. Freeze overnight, or for at least 4 hours.

3. These smoothie pops will keep in the freezer for up to 6 weeks.

FROZEN YOGHURT BARK

| Each recipe serves 4 | Prep time: 5–10 minutes | Freezing time: 2–3 hours |

This delicious frozen treat is easy to make and requires no special equipment. All you need is yoghurt, honey and toppings of your choice. Simple, tasty and super-healthy, too.

TUTTI FRUTTI FROZEN YOGHURT BARK

Ingredients

400g plain Greek yoghurt

2 tbsp honey

150g mixed chopped fruit
(I like to use peaches, strawberries, raspberries, kiwis and blueberries)

Method

1. Line a large baking dish with foil.

2. Mix together the yoghurt and honey in a bowl and spread the mixture out in the lined dish.

3. Top the yoghurt-honey mixture with the chopped fruit then freeze for 2–3 hours until solid.

4. Remove the yoghurt bark from the freezer and break it up or cut it into pieces.

5. Serve immediately or store in a freezer bag for up to 1 month.

CHOCOLATE NUT FROZEN YOGHURT BARK

Ingredients

400g plain Greek yoghurt

2 tbsp honey

20g salted peanuts

20g milk or dark chocolate, melted

Method

1. Line a large baking dish with foil.

2. Mix together the yoghurt and honey in a bowl and spread the mixture out in the lined dish.

3. Scatter the peanuts on top and drizzle with the melted chocolate. Freeze for 2–3 hours until solid.

4. Remove the yoghurt bark from the freezer and break it up or cut it into pieces.

5. Serve immediately or store in a freezer bag for up to 1 month.

POPSICLES

| Each recipe makes 6 popsicles | Prep time: 5–10 minutes | Freezing time: overnight |

Whatever the season, you can use fruit to flavour and sweeten these delicious popsicles. They're all really easy to make and will keep in the freezer for up to 8 weeks.

MANGO AND COCONUT POPSICLES

Ingredients

400g tin coconut milk

2 tbsp honey

1 tsp vanilla extract

1 mango, peeled, stoned and cut into pieces

2 tbsp desiccated coconut

Method

1. Put the coconut milk, honey and vanilla extract into a large jug and whisk to combine.

2. Pour the mixture into 6 popsicle moulds, tap them on a hard surface to remove any air, then place in the freezer for 30–60 minutes until firm but not hard.

3. Put the mango flesh in a blender and blitz until smooth. Pour the mango purée into the popsicle moulds, on top of the coconut. Add a stick to each mould and return to the freezer overnight.

4. Remove the popsicles from the freezer. You may need to leave them out or run the moulds under cold water to remove the popsicles. Sprinkle the popsicles with the desiccated coconut and serve immediately.

WATERMELON AND KIWI POPSICLES

Ingredients

400g seedless watermelon

2 kiwis, peeled

Method

1. Put the watermelon into a blender, blitz until smooth pour into 6 popsicle moulds, filling each mould about three-quarters full. Tap them on a hard surface to remove any air, then place in the freezer for 1 hour.

2. Put the kiwis in a blender and blitz until smooth. Pour the kiwi purée into the popsicle moulds on top of the watermelon. Add a stick to each mould and return to the freezer overnight.

3. Remove the popsicles from the freezer. Leave them out or run them under cold water to remove the moulds.

STRAWBERRY AND CHOCOLATE POPSICLES

Ingredients

150g strawberries, hulled

270g plain yoghurt

1 tbsp honey

1 tsp vanilla extract

50g milk or dark chocolate

Method

1. Put the strawberries, yoghurt, honey and vanilla extract into a blender and blitz until smooth.

2. Pour the mixture into 6 popsicle moulds and tap the bottom of the moulds on the work surface to remove any air bubbles. Add a stick to each mould and freeze overnight.

3. Remove the popsicles from the freezer. You may need to leave them out or run the moulds under cold water to remove the popsicles.

4. Melt the chocolate and drizzle it over the popsicles. Serve immediately.

FRUIT SALAD POPSICLES

Ingredients

1 peach, peeled and cut into thin slices

1 kiwi, peeled and cut into thin slices

10 blueberries, halved

6 raspberries, halved or quartered

6 strawberries, hulled and thinly sliced

150ml apple juice

Method

1. Divide the sliced fruit between 6 popsicle moulds, pressing some of the fruit pieces against the inside of the moulds.

2. Fill the moulds with the apple juice, add a stick to each mould and freeze overnight.

3. Remove the popsicles from the freezer. You may need to leave them out or run the moulds under cold water to remove the popsicles.

NICE-CREAM

   KM

| Each recipe serves 4 | Prep time: 10 minutes | Freezing time: 5 hours |

Nice-cream, made by blending frozen bananas, is a really great alternative to traditional ice cream and is completely dairy-free, too (although I do include a choc-chip variation). Simply blend frozen bananas with your choice of flavourings.

CHOCOLATE ORANGE NICE-CREAM

Ingredients

4 ripe bananas

2 tsp cocoa powder

2 tsp honey

juice of 2 oranges

Method

1. Peel the bananas and cut each banana into 6–8 slices. Place in a freezer bag and freeze for a minimum of 5 hours until solid.

2. Remove the bananas from the freezer and put them into a food processor. Blitz for a few minutes until the bananas start to break down, then add the cocoa powder, honey and orange juice and blitz again until it has the consistency of ice cream. Be careful not to over-blitz though, which would cause the bananas to melt.

3. Serve immediately or transfer the ice cream to a container and store in the freezer for up to 1 month.

PEANUT BUTTER NICE-CREAM

Ingredients

4 ripe bananas

100g crunchy peanut butter

Method

1. Peel the bananas and cut each banana into 6–8 slices. Place in a freezer bag and freeze for a minimum of 5 hours until solid.

2. Remove the bananas from the freezer and put them into a food processor. Blitz for a few minutes until the bananas start to break down, then add the peanut butter and blitz again until it has the consistency of ice cream. Be careful not to over-blitz though, which would cause the bananas to melt.

3. Serve immediately or transfer the ice cream to a container and store in the freezer for up to 1 month.

RASPBERRY RIPPLE NICE-CREAM

Ingredients

4 ripe bananas

½ tsp vanilla extract

100g fresh raspberries

Method

1. Peel the bananas and cut each banana into 6–8 slices. Place in a freezer bag and freeze for a minimum of 5 hours until solid.

2. Remove the bananas from the freezer and put them into a food processor with the vanilla extract. Blitz until it has the consistency of ice cream. Be careful not to over-blitz though, which would cause the bananas to melt.

3. Add the raspberries and stir them in with a spoon to get a ripple effect through the ice cream.

4. Serve immediately or transfer the ice cream to a container and store in the freezer for up to 1 month.

MINT CHOC CHIP NICE-CREAM

Ingredients

4 ripe bananas

50g fresh spinach

10 mint leaves

50g milk or dark chocolate chips

Method

1. Peel the bananas and cut each banana into 6–8 slices. Place in a freezer bag and freeze for a minimum of 5 hours until solid.

2. Remove the bananas from the freezer and put them into a food processor. Blitz for a few minutes until the bananas start to break down, then add the spinach and mint leaves and blitz again until it has the consistency of ice cream. Be careful not to over-blitz though, which would cause the bananas to melt.

3. Add the chocolate chips and stir with a spoon.

4. Serve immediately or transfer the ice cream to a container and store in the freezer for up to 1 month.

BREAD AND CRACKERS

Having a few good sweet and savoury breads, crackers and breadstick recipes
is always useful as you can serve them up in so many ways. Add slices
of the bread to lunchboxes, serve the crackers with a family
lunch or pack the breadsticks into your bag for
an instant toddler snack on the go.

VEGETABLE CORNBREAD

| Makes: 1 loaf (about 16 slices) | Prep time: 10 minutes | Cook time: 1 hour 10 minutes |

Cornbread is a tasty, dense bread made with polenta or cornmeal. It gives
a delicious flavour to the bread, along with a very subtle crunchy texture.
I've flavoured mine with bacon, cheese and lots of vegetables.

Ingredients

150g bacon lardons

100g grated carrot

125g grated courgette

100g broccoli, chopped

50g fresh spinach

½ red pepper, chopped

1 spring onion, chopped

175g plain flour

175g polenta

2 tsp baking powder

2 eggs

250ml milk

100g unsalted butter, melted,
  plus extra for greasing

75g grated Cheddar cheese

salt and pepper, to taste

Method

1. Preheat the oven to 200°C/180°C Fan/Gas Mark 6.
   Grease a 900g (2lb) loaf tin and line it with baking
   parchment.

2. Heat a frying pan over a medium heat, add the bacon
   lardons and fry for 4 minutes until crispy. Add the carrot,
   courgette, broccoli, spinach, red pepper and spring onion
   and fry for a further 3-4 minutes until the vegetables
   are soft.

3. Mix the flour, polenta and baking powder in a large bowl.
   Add the eggs, milk, melted butter and grated cheese
   and mix well.

4. Add the bacon and vegetables, season with a little salt
   and pepper and stir one final time.

5. Pour the mixture into the prepared loaf tin and bake
   in the oven for 1 hour.

6. Allow the cornbread to cool in the tin for 5-10 minutes
   then turn it out onto a wire rack and let it cool for
   a little longer.

7. The cornbread will keep in the fridge for up to 3 days
   or can be sliced and frozen for up to 1 month.

SWEET AND SAVOURY PASTRY STRAWS

| Makes: 16 straws (8 sweet and 8 savoury) | Prep time: 10 minutes | Cook time: 10–12 minutes |

Easy to make and fun for the kids to get involved with, these pastry straws can be made either sweet or savoury, or a combination of both (as shown here).

Ingredients

320g ready-rolled sheet of puff pastry

2 tbsp pesto (see page 78 for my Popeye's Protein Pesto)

1 tbsp Raspberry Chia Jam (see page 179) or your favourite jam

Method

1. Preheat the oven to 220°C/200°C Fan/Gas Mark 7 and line 2 baking trays with baking parchment.

2. Unroll the pastry and cut it in half widthways and then in half again so that you have 4 equal-sized rectangles.

3. Spread the pesto onto one piece of pastry and place another piece of pastry on top of that.

4. Spread the jam onto the third piece of pastry and place the last piece of pastry on top.

5. Cut each of the pieces of pastry into 8 long strips. Then twist and place on the lined baking trays – the jam straws on one tray and the pesto straws on the other.

6. Bake in the oven for 10–12 minutes until the straws are golden brown.

7. Remove from the oven and allow to cool before serving. They are best eaten the same day they are made, but will keep in an airtight container at room temperature for up to 24 hours.

SEEDED OATCAKES

| Makes: 30–40 oatcakes | Prep time: 15 minutes | Cook time: 17–19 minutes |

Oatcakes may seem a little boring, but they make the perfect base for lots of healthy toppings. Try them with a slice of cheese and tomato or for a sweet snack spread with some homemade Chocolate-hazelnut Spread (see page 183). Delicious!

Ingredients

200g rolled oats

75g plain flour, plus extra
  for dusting

½ tsp bicarbonate of soda

80g unsalted butter, softened

80ml cold water

2 tbsp small seeds (poppy seeds,
  sesame seeds, linseeds, etc.)

Method

1. Preheat the oven to 200°C/180°C Fan/Gas Mark 6 and line 2 baking trays with baking parchment.

2. Put the oats into a food processor and blitz to break them down to a coarse flour. Add the plain flour, bicarbonate of soda and butter and blitz again. Add a little of the water at a time, blitzing continuously, until it forms a dough (you don't want the dough to be too sticky). Add the seeds and mix them in with a spoon.

3. Turn the dough out onto a lightly floured surface and roll it out until it is about 2.5mm thick.

4. Use a 5cm or 6cm plain round cutter to cut out 30-40 oatcakes. Place them on the lined baking trays and bake in the oven for 17–19 minutes until golden brown.

5. Remove from the oven and leave to cool on the trays to crisp up. The oatcakes will keep in an airtight container for up to 3 days.

6. If you don't want to use all the dough at once, wrap it in cling film, put it in a freezer bag and store it in the freezer for up to 3 months.

CHEESY CHEDDAR CRACKERS

| Makes: 40–50 crackers | Prep time: 15 minutes | Cook time: 15 minutes |

These cheesy Cheddar crackers are incredibly moreish and perfect for popping into lunchboxes or snack packs for peckish kids! They are easy to make too and a great way to get kids helping out in the kitchen.

Ingredients

120g plain flour, plus extra for dusting

60g unsalted butter

170g grated Cheddar cheese

20g grated Parmesan cheese

½ tsp smoked paprika

50ml cold water

Method

1. Preheat the oven to 200°C/180°C Fan/Gas Mark 6 and line 2 baking trays with baking parchment.

2. Put the flour, butter, grated cheeses and smoked paprika into a food processor. Add a little of the water and blitz until the ingredients form a dough. Add more of the water if necessary.

3. Roll the dough out on a floured surface until it is about 2.5mm thick. Use a 4cm or 5cm round cutter to cut out 40-50 circles and place them on the lined baking trays.

4. Prick the top of the crackers with a fork then bake in the oven for 15 minutes.

5. Remove from the oven and leave the crackers to cool and crisp up on the trays.

6. The crackers will keep in an airtight container for up to 3 days.

GARLIC AND HERB BREADSTICKS

   GF DF BC FR

| Makes: 50–60 breadsticks | Prep time: 30 minutes | Cook time: 15–17 minutes |

Breadsticks make a really great snack for kids, served with some dip
and raw veggies on the side. Make a big batch at a time
or freeze the dough to use another day.

Ingredients

450g wholemeal flour, plus
extra for dusting

1 x 7g sachet of fast-action
dried yeast

1 tsp fine salt

2 tsp dried Italian herbs

1 tsp garlic powder

1½ tbsp extra virgin olive oil

300ml lukewarm water

Method

1. Preheat the oven to 220°C/200°C Fan/Gas Mark 7
   and line 2 baking trays with baking parchment.

2. Put the flour, yeast, salt, dried herbs, garlic powder
   and oil into a bowl. Add a little of the water and mix
   until the dough becomes soft but not sticky.

3. Knead the dough for about 5 minutes. You can do
   this by hand or in a stand mixer fitted with the
   dough hook attachment.

4. Take a tablespoon-sized piece of the dough and
   use your hands to roll it into a long strip on a lightly
   floured surface.

5. Cut the strip in half and place onto one of the lined
   baking trays. You can make all the breadsticks at once
   (the dough will make 50–60 breadsticks) or just use
   what you need, wrap the rest of the dough in cling film,
   place in a freezer bag and freeze for up to 3 months.

6. Place the trays of breadsticks somewhere warm
   for 15 minutes, uncovered, then bake in the oven
   for 15–17 minutes until crisp.

7. Remove from the oven and leave to cool.

8. The breadsticks will keep for up to 2 days in an airtight
   container or can be frozen for up to 3 months.

SWEET THINGS AND DRINKS

DESSERTS AND CAKES

No matter how much my daughter eats for dinner, she always asks, 'What's for pudding, Mum?!' Some days it's yoghurt and fruit, but other days I treat her to some homemade cake or crumble.

These recipes are ideal to make at the weekend when you have a little more time to devote to baking. They are perfect for family lunches or to take to a friend's house for the ultimate playdate treat!

NO-SUGAR RICE PUDDING

| Serves: 4 | Prep time: 2 minutes | Cook time: 25–30 minutes |

A delicious sugar-free rice pudding recipe, naturally sweetened with coconut and topped with fresh fruit.

Ingredients

200g pudding rice

400ml coconut milk (from a carton)

400ml whole milk

1 tbsp desiccated coconut

1 tsp vanilla extract

100g chopped strawberries or raspberries, to serve

Method

1. Put all the ingredients, except the berries, into a large heavy-based saucepan.

2. Bring to the boil over a medium heat then reduce the heat, cover and simmer for 25–30 minutes, or until all the milk has been absorbed and the rice is soft, stirring it every few minutes.

3. Remove from the heat and serve warm with chopped berries on top or keep in an airtight container in the fridge for up to 2 days.

HEALTHIER ETON MESS

| Serves: 4 | Prep time: 5 minutes |

A healthier take on this classic British dessert, using Greek yoghurt and just a small amount of cream.

Ingredients

150ml double cream

300g plain Greek yoghurt

1 tbsp honey

75g meringue

300g strawberries, hulled and chopped

Method

1. Whip the cream in a large bowl until thick. Fold in the yoghurt and honey and mix with a spoon.

2. Crumble in pieces of meringue then fold in the chopped strawberries.

3. Transfer the mixture into 4 bowls or jars.

4. Serve immediately or keep in the fridge for up to 6 hours.

CHOCOLATE ORANGE TART

| Serves: 8 | Prep time: 15 minutes | Cook time: 5 minutes, plus 3 hours in the fridge |

Chocolate and orange have to be one of the best food combinations ever, and this tart combines both of those in a delicious but also super-nutritious dessert.

Ingredients

For the base
100g pitted dates

175g mixed unsalted nuts (I use pecans, almonds and cashews)

2 tbsp coconut oil

1 tbsp cocoa powder

1 tsp vanilla extract

For the filling
4 sheets of gelatine

400g tin coconut milk

juice of 4 oranges (about 200ml)

1 tsp grated orange zest

40g milk or dark chocolate

Method

1. Put the tin of coconut milk upside down in the fridge overnight.

2. Put the dates in a heatproof bowl, cover with boiling water and leave for about 10 minutes to soften them.

3. Drain the dates and put them into a food processor with the nuts, coconut oil, cocoa powder and vanilla extract. Blitz until all the ingredients have combined.

4. Press the base mixture evenly into the base of a 23cm round tart tin and place in the freezer for 15 minutes to firm up.

5. Meanwhile, follow the instructions on the gelatine packet to soften the sheets of gelatine, then put them into a saucepan.

6. Remove the tin of coconut milk from the fridge, turn it the right way round and open it. Scoop out the creamy coconut and add it to the saucepan, leaving the coconut water behind. Add the orange juice and zest and cook over a low heat for 4–5 minutes until the coconut cream has completely dissolved.

7. Remove from the heat, let it cool a little then pour the mixture on top of the nut base. Put in the fridge for 3–4 hours until the filling has set.

8. Melt the chocolate and drizzle or swirl it on top of the tart, then cut the tart into 8 slices.

9. The tart will keep in the fridge, covered, for up to 3 days.

RHUBARB AND STRAWBERRY CUSTARD POTS

| Serves: 4 | Prep time: 5 minutes | Cook time: 10 minutes |

Early summer is the perfect time to enjoy rhubarb and strawberries. Use these simple seasonal fruits to create a tangy dessert topped with homemade vanilla custard.

Ingredients

For the rhubarb

300g fresh rhubarb, chopped

150g fresh or frozen strawberries, halved

2 tbsp honey

juice of 1 clementine

50ml water

For the custard

500ml whole milk

2 tbsp honey

1 tsp vanilla extract

4 egg yolks

2 tbsp cornflour

Method

1. Put the chopped rhubarb, chopped strawberries, honey, clementine juice and water into a large saucepan. Bring to the boil over a medium heat, then reduce the heat to low and simmer for about 10 minutes until the liquid has evaporated and the fruit has softened and cooked down.

2. Meanwhile, gently heat the milk, honey and vanilla in another heavy-based saucepan.

3. Whisk the egg yolks and cornflour together in a jug then gradually add this mixture to the milk.

4. Continue to cook over a low heat for about 5 minutes until the custard has thickened, whisking constantly to stop lumps forming.

5. Divide the custard between 4 bowls or cups and add the stewed rhubarb on top. The rhubarb and custard will keep separately in the fridge for up to 3 days and can be served cold or reheated in the microwave.

PEANUT BUTTER BROWNIES

| Makes: 9 brownies | Prep time: 10 minutes | Cook time: 15 minutes |

Chocolatey fudgy peanut-butter brownies made with a very secret ingredient...black beans!
Packed with fibre and protein, these brownies are sure to keep kids happy and full!

Ingredients

230g tin or carton cooked
   black beans, drained

115g smooth peanut butter

50g coconut oil, melted

50g honey

50ml milk

1 egg

1 tsp vanilla extract

100g plain flour

40g soft light brown sugar
   or coconut sugar

20g cocoa powder

½ tsp baking powder

¼ tsp bicarbonate of soda

Method

1. Preheat the oven to 200°C/180°C Fan/Gas Mark 6
   and line a brownie tin (about 25 x 22cm) with baking
   parchment.

2. Put the drained black beans, 75g of the peanut butter,
   the oil, honey, milk, egg and vanilla extract into a food
   processor and blitz until all the ingredients are well
   combined.

3. Put the flour, sugar, cocoa powder, baking powder
   and bicarbonate of soda into a large bowl and mix
   with a spoon.

4. Add the wet ingredients to the dry ingredients and
   mix just enough to combine them.

5. Transfer the mixture to the prepared tin and bake
   in the oven for 12 minutes.

6. Melt the remaining peanut butter in bowl in the
   microwave then drizzle it over the top of the brownies.
   Return them to the oven for a further 3 minutes.

7. Remove from the oven and leave the brownies to cool
   in the tin slightly before lifting them out and leaving
   them to cool further. Cut into 9 portions.

8. The brownies will keep in an airtight container
   in the fridge for up to 4 days.

RASPBERRY CHIA CRUMBLE SQUARES

| Makes: 9 squares | Prep time: 10 minutes | Cook time: 20 minutes |

All the taste of a crumble but in easy-to-eat squares instead! Made with raspberry chia jam this treat is lower in sugar than your average dessert.

Ingredients

150g plain flour

75g rolled oats

100g unsalted butter, melted, plus extra for greasing

50g soft light brown sugar or coconut sugar

1 tbsp honey

1 tsp vanilla extract

½ tsp ground cinnamon

½ tsp bicarbonate of soda

150g Raspberry Chia Jam (see page 179)

½ tsp cornflour

Method

1. Preheat the oven to 190°C/170°C Fan/Gas Mark 5 and generously grease a square baking dish or baking tin (about 20cm).

2. Put the flour, oats, melted butter, sugar, honey, vanilla extract, cinnamon and bicarbonate of soda into a large bowl and mix together until well combined.

3. Transfer half of the mixture to the baking dish and press it down firmly to make it as compact as possible.

4. Bake in the oven for 5 minutes and then remove.

5. Mix the jam and cornflour together in a bowl. Spread this evenly on top of the crumble base.

6. Use your hands to add the remaining crumble mixture on top of the jam and gently press down.

7. Bake in the oven for a further 15 minutes.

8. Remove from the oven and leave the crumble to cool in the dish before removing it and cutting it into 9 squares.

9. The squares will keep in an airtight container in the fridge for up to 3 days. They can be eaten cold or warmed in the microwave.

FINN'S SWEET POTATO CHOCOLATE CAKE

| Serves: 6 | Prep time: 10 minutes | Cook time: 20–25 minutes |

This is my son's favourite homemade cake. In fact, the first time I made it I left it to cool on a wire rack in the kitchen. I went outside into the garden and came back to find him and the cake on the floor, and most of it eaten!

Ingredients

200g cooked and mashed
  sweet potato

100g apple sauce (see page 186
  for my homemade apple sauce)

80g coconut oil or unsalted butter,
  melted, plus extra for greasing

1 tsp vanilla extract

60g plain flour

60g wholemeal flour

30g soft light brown sugar
  or coconut sugar

25g cocoa powder

1 tsp baking powder

1 tsp bicarbonate of soda

50g milk or dark chocolate chips

plain Greek yoghurt, raspberries
  and blueberries, to serve

Method

1. Preheat the oven to 200°C/180°C Fan/Gas Mark 6. Grease a 22cm round cake tin and line it with baking parchment.

2. Put the mashed sweet potato, apple sauce, melted coconut oil or butter and vanilla extract into a bowl and mix together.

3. Put the plain and wholemeal flours, light brown or coconut sugar, cocoa powder, baking powder and bicarbonate of soda into a second, larger bowl and mix well, then stir in the chocolate chips.

4. Add the wet ingredients to the dry ingredients and stir until all the ingredients have combined.

5. Pour the cake mixture into the prepared tin and bake in the oven for 20–25 minutes until a skewer inserted into the middle of the cake comes out clean.

6. Remove from the oven, leave to cool in the tin for 10 minutes, then transfer to a wire rack to cool completely.

7. Serve with Greek yoghurt and berries.

AOIFE'S CARROT CAKE

| Serves: 10 | Prep time: 15 minutes | Cook time: 25 minutes |

My daughter absolutely loves carrot cake, which is surprising for a fussy eater given that there are so many 'bits' in it! I make this healthier version at home, sweetened with honey and apple sauce, and it always goes down a treat.

Ingredients

For the cake

2 eggs

100g unsalted butter, melted, plus extra for greasing

150g apple sauce (see page 186 for my homemade apple sauce)

75g honey

1 tsp vanilla extract

400g grated carrots

300g plain flour

2 tsp baking powder

1 tsp bicarbonate of soda

1 tsp ground cinnamon

75g walnuts, roughly chopped

50g raisins

grated zest of 1 clementine

For the icing

200g cream cheese

25g unsalted butter, softened

grated zest and juice of 1 clementine

½ tsp vanilla extract

Method

1. Preheat the oven to 200°C/180°C Fan/Gas Mark 6. Grease two 20cm round cake tins and line them with baking parchment.

2. Whisk the eggs in a bowl until light and fluffy. Add the melted butter, apple sauce, honey and vanilla extract and fold them gently into the eggs to avoid knocking out too much air. Add the grated carrots and leave the bowl to one side for 5-10 minutes to allow the carrot to soften.

3. Meanwhile, mix the flour, baking powder, bicarbonate of soda and cinnamon in a large bowl with a spoon. Add the carrot mixture to the flour mixture, along with the walnuts, raisins and clementine zest and mix again.

4. Divide the cake mixture between the prepared cake tins then bake in the oven for 25-30 minutes until a skewer inserted into the middle of each cake comes out clean.

5. Remove from the oven and leave the cakes to cool a little in the tins before turning them out onto a wire rack to cool completely.

6. To make the icing, beat the cream cheese and butter in a bowl until smooth, add the clementine zest and juice and vanilla and beat again.

7. Place one of the carrot cakes on a plate or cake stand and spread half of the cream cheese icing on top. Add the second cake on top then cover it with the remaining icing.

8. Put the cake in the fridge for 10 minutes to firm up, then serve. Keep in the fridge in an airtight container for up to 2 days.

DRINKS

Water is vitally important for a growing child and encouraging kids to drink it freely from an early age will be massively beneficial for the rest of their childhood. While other types of drinks cannot and should not replace water completely, they can count towards a child's daily fluid intake.

FLAVOURED WATER

| Each recipe serves 4 | Prep time: 2 minutes |

A lot of children simply do not like the taste of plain water and for this reason it can be a real struggle moving them away from squash and fruit juice. Experiment with flavouring your own water using fruit, veggies and herbs. It will keep in a jug in the fridge for 1 day.

LIME AND CUCUMBER WATER

Ingredients

1 litre still or sparkling water

1 lime, sliced

¼ cucumber, sliced

STRAWBERRY AND BASIL WATER

Ingredients

1 litre still or sparkling water

10 strawberries, halved

5 basil leaves

ORANGE AND KIWI WATER

Ingredients

1 litre still or sparkling water

1 orange, sliced

1 kiwi, peeled and sliced

BLUEBERRY AND MINT WATER

Ingredients

1 litre still or sparkling water

20 blueberries, left whole

5 mint leaves

FLAVOURED MILK

| Each recipe serves 2 | Prep time: 2 minutes |

Just a little flavouring can turn a standard glass of milk into a really tasty drink. Just put all the ingredients into a blender and blitz until smooth. The milk will keep in the fridge for up to 2 days, although it may separate, so give it a good shake before drinking.

STRAWBERRY MILK

Ingredients

500ml milk (dairy or non-dairy)

100g fresh or frozen strawberries

½ tsp vanilla extract

BANANA MILK

Ingredients

500ml milk (dairy or non-dairy)

1 banana

½ tsp vanilla extract

CHOCOLATE MILK

Ingredients

500ml milk (dairy or non-dairy)

1 tbsp cocoa powder

2 tsp honey

CHOCOLATE-HAZELNUT MILK

Ingredients

500ml milk (dairy or non-dairy)

2 tbsp Chocolate-hazelnut Spread (see page 183)

1 tbsp cocoa powder

HEALTHY STRAWBERRY LEMONADE

| Serves: 2 | Prep time: 2 minutes |

A healthier homemade strawberry lemonade that is perfect for summer
and can be made with either still or sparkling water.

Ingredients

100g frozen strawberries

500ml still or sparkling water

1 tsp honey

juice of 1 lemon

handful of ice cubes

Method

1. Put all the ingredients into a blender and blitz until smooth.

2. This lemonade is best served immediately.

CARROT AND ORANGE SMOOTHIE

| Serves: 2 | Prep time: 2 minutes |

A super-refreshing smoothie, packed with fruits and veggies, that tastes
like summer even if the weather outside says otherwise!

Ingredients

150g carrots, chopped

100ml cold water

100g plain yoghurt (dairy
   or non-dairy)

juice of 2 oranges (about 100ml)

½ tsp grated orange zest

handful of ice cubes

Method

1. Put the carrots and water into a blender and blitz until smooth.

2. Add the yoghurt, orange juice and zest and some ice cubes and blitz again.

3. Pour the smoothie through a fine sieve to remove the grainy bits of carrots.

4. This smoothie is best served immediately.

GREEN SMOOTHIE

| Serves: 2 | Prep time: 2 minutes |

A simple but delicious smoothie that is packed full of goodness and tastes super-sweet. The coconut water also makes it a really hydrating drink, perfect for hot days.

Ingredients

500ml coconut water

200g frozen tropical fruit
(I use frozen mango and pineapple)

50g spinach

Method

1. Put all the ingredients into a blender and blitz until smooth.

2. This smoothie is best served immediately.

QUINOA SMOOTHIE

| Serves: 2 | Prep time: 2 minutes |

A protein-packed smoothie made with quinoa, yoghurt and berries. A delicious and healthy drink that can be served with breakfast or as part of an afternoon snack.

Ingredients

200ml milk (dairy
or non-dairy)

100g plain yoghurt (dairy
or non-dairy)

1 banana

250g mixed frozen berries

100g cooked quinoa
(30g uncooked)

1 tsp honey

Method

1. Put all the ingredients into a blender and blitz until smooth.

2. This smoothie is best served immediately.

FRUITY PARTY SLUSHIES

| Serves: 10 (5 small glasses per fruit) | Prep time: 10 minutes |

These watermelon and pineapple slushies are such a simple but
fun way to serve healthy drinks at a kids' party.

Ingredients

1 large watermelon (seedless
if possible)

2 limes

1 large bag of ice cubes

1 large pineapple

Method

1. Chop the top off the watermelon and scoop out
   all the flesh. I find using an ice cream scoop is the
   easiest way to do this.

2. Put the seedless watermelon flesh into a blender with
   the juice of the 2 limes and a large handful of ice cubes.
   Blitz until smooth, then pour the mixture back into the
   watermelon. Leave any extra aside in a jug.

3. Quickly rinse out the blender and do the same
   to the pineapple, chopping the top off, scooping out
   the flesh and adding it to the blender with some ice.

4. Again, pour this into the pineapple, putting any extra
   aside in a jug to fill up later.

5. Add some colourful straws and cocktail umbrellas
   to the slushies and serve immediately.

GINGERBREAD HOT CHOCOLATE

| Serves: 4 | Prep time: 3 minutes |

Cosy up on the sofa on a winter's evening with a mug of this warming gingerbread hot chocolate. The spices used are very mild to suit young palates but feel free to double the quantities for more flavour.

Ingredients

1 litre milk (dairy or non-dairy)

2 tbsp cocoa powder

1 tbsp honey

1 tsp vanilla extract

½ tsp ground ginger

½ tsp ground cinnamon

¼ tsp freshly grated or ground nutmeg

whipped cream and chocolate shavings, to serve (optional)

Method

1. Put all the ingredients into a large saucepan over a low heat. Gently heat the milk until it is warm but not boiling.

2. Remove from the heat and divide between 4 mugs. Top with some whipped cream and chocolate shavings, if using.

DIPS AND SAUCES

SWEET

My children love sweet spreads like jam, peanut butter and chocolate spread.
Making your own versions at home is easier than you think and a lot healthier too,
with less sugar and no artificial additives. You can make other flavours of jam
using your favourite fruits or use different nuts to create various
nut butters using my Peanut Butter recipe. Experiment
and see what you and your family enjoy.

RASPBERRY CHIA JAM

| Makes: a 250g jar | Prep time: 2 minutes | Cook time: 10 minutes |

A delicious refined-sugar-free alternative to jam, made from
raspberries and thickened with chia seeds.

Ingredients

250g fresh or frozen raspberries

1 tbsp honey

½ tsp vanilla extract

1½ tbsp chia seeds

Method

1. Put the raspberries into a saucepan over a medium heat. Using a potato masher, press down on the raspberries as they begin to heat up. If they are not very juicy, add a splash of water to help them break down.

2. When the raspberries have broken down to a sauce consistency, add the honey and vanilla and stir until combined. Remove from the heat and allow the mixture to cool a little then add the chia seeds.

3. Transfer the 'jam' to a clean jar and allow it to cool completely. Once it has reached room temperature transfer it to the fridge for 1 hour to set.

4. Store in an airtight jar in the fridge for up to 1 week.

PEANUT BUTTER

| Makes: a 300g jar | Prep time: 10 minutes | Cook time: 15 minutes |

This healthy peanut butter is super-easy to make and will keep in
an airtight container in the fridge for up to 1 week.

Ingredients

300g unsalted, shelled peanuts

50g coconut oil, melted

1 tbsp honey

pinch of salt

Method

1. Preheat the oven to 200°C/180°C Fan/Gas Mark 6
   and spread the peanuts out on a baking tray. Roast
   the peanuts for 15 minutes to help release the oils.

2. Remove from the oven and allow the nuts to cool
   then transfer to a food processor along with the
   melted coconut oil. Blitz for 5 minutes until smooth.

3. Add the honey and salt and blitz again – it should
   thicken up. Transfer to a clean jar and allow to cool.

SUNFLOWER BUTTER

| Makes: a 400g jar | Prep time: 15 minutes | Cook time: 4 minutes |

This sunflower butter makes a great alternative to peanut butter in lots of my snack
recipes. It will keep in an airtight container in the fridge for up to 1 week.

Ingredients

300g sunflower seeds

50g coconut oil, melted

3 tbsp honey

1 tsp vanilla extract

pinch of salt

100–150ml cold water

Method

1. Put the sunflower seeds into a large saucepan or wok
   and dry-fry over a medium heat for 3–4 minutes. Allow
   the seeds to cool a little, then transfer them to a food
   processor with the melted coconut oil and blitz until
   smooth. This will take about 10 minutes, so keep going!

2. Add the honey, vanilla extract and pinch of salt and
   give it one final blitz. The mixture will thicken up a lot
   so add a little of the water until you get the right
   consistency. Transfer to a clean jar and allow to cool.

CHOCOLATE-HAZELNUT SPREAD

| Makes: a 350g jar | Prep time: 15 minutes | Cook time: 8 minutes |

Ditch the sugary shop-bought variety and make your own delicious
and healthy chocolate-hazelnut spread at home instead.

Ingredients

250g hazelnuts

30g coconut oil, melted

2 tbsp cocoa powder

2 tbsp honey

1 tsp vanilla extract

pinch of salt

150ml milk (optional)

Method

1. Preheat the oven to 200°C/180°C Fan/Gas Mark 6
   and spread the hazelnuts out on a baking tray.
   Roast the nuts for 8 minutes.

2. Remove from the oven, place the hazelnuts onto
   a clean tea towel, fold the towel over them and
   rub until most of the skins have come off the nuts.

3. Transfer the nuts to a food processor, add the melted
   coconut oil and blitz for about 5 minutes until smooth.

4. Add the cocoa powder, honey, vanilla extract and
   salt and blitz again until the mixture has a smooth
   paste consistency.

5. If you have a very high-powered food processor
   you will be able to blitz the ingredients to a spread
   consistency. If you need to thin the mixture out a little
   then gradually add the milk, a little at a time, blitzing
   continuously until it reaches a spreadable consistency.

6. Transfer to a clean jar and allow to cool.

7. Store in the fridge for up to 1 week. If the spread
   solidifies in the fridge, reheat it gently in the microwave
   for about 30 seconds until you get the right consistency
   for spreading.

SAVOURY

My family loves a condiment – ketchup, mayo and lots of dips all feature regularly at our dinner table. I often make my own; knowing exactly what I've put into them means I don't feel as bad when veggies are dipped in homemade ketchup!

EASY MAYONNAISE

| Makes: a 250g jar | Prep time: 2 minutes |

This is the easiest mayonnaise ever! With just five ingredients and one jar, it can be whipped up in a couple of minutes and will keep in a sealed jar in the fridge for up to 1 week.

Ingredients

250ml mild and light
  olive oil

1 egg

½ tsp English mustard
  powder

½ tsp salt

juice of ½–1 lemon

Method

1. Pour a little of the olive oil into a large jar. Add the egg, mustard powder and salt and begin to blend with a hand-held blender.

2. Once those ingredients have combined, slowly drizzle in the rest of the olive oil while the blender is still running. The slower you do this the more likely it is that the egg and oil will emulsify correctly.

3. Once all the olive oil has been incorporated, add the lemon juice to taste and serve.

KIDDIE KETCHUP

| Makes: a 300ml jar | Prep time: 1 minute | Cook time: 15 minutes |

If, like mine, your kids eat ketchup with everything then try making your own. It can be kept in an airtight container in the fridge for up to 2 weeks or frozen for up to 3 months.

Ingredients

500g passata

3 tbsp white wine vinegar

3 tbsp tomato purée

2 tbsp honey

½ tsp Dijon mustard

salt and pepper, to taste

Method

1. Put all the ingredients, except the seasoning, into a saucepan, bring to the boil over a medium heat then reduce the heat and simmer, covered (it will splatter!), for 15 minutes. Remove from the heat and season.

2. Allow the ketchup to cool before storing in an airtight container.

APPLE SAUCE

GF DF BC FR

| Makes: a 600g jar | Prep time: 5 minutes | Cook time: 20 minutes |

Shop-bought apple sauce usually contains sugar along with gelling agents and other preservatives. Make your own at home with just apples and water – super-simple. It's great to make in bulk and keep in the freezer.

Ingredients

650g red apples (about 6)

200ml water if skins left on, 150ml if skins peeled off

Method

1. Chop the apples and remove the cores. You can leave the skins on if you like. I prefer to leave them on as it is easier, plus you are not losing the nutrition. However, bear in mind that the apple sauce will have a slight pink colour if the skins are left on.

2. Put the chopped apples into a large saucepan and add the water. Bring to the boil over a medium heat, then reduce the heat and simmer for about 20 minutes, or until the water has evaporated and the apples are soft.

3. Transfer the apples to a stand blender or food processor and blitz until smooth.

4. The apple sauce will keep in an airtight container in the fridge for up to 5 days and can be frozen for up to 3 months.

SWEET CHILLI SAUCE

| Makes: a 250g jar | Prep time: 1 minute | Cook time: 7 minutes |

You might think your kids will hate anything strongly flavoured or spicy
but give this sweet chilli sauce a go and they might surprise you.
It's quite mild and is great served as a dipping sauce.

Ingredients

2 red peppers, halved,
    deseeded and chopped

½ red chilli, deseeded
    and finely diced

2 tbsp white wine vinegar

2 tbsp honey

1 garlic clove, crushed

100ml water

1 tbsp cornflour

Method

1. Put the red pepper, chilli, white wine vinegar, honey,
   garlic and water into a small saucepan and bring to the
   boil over a medium heat, then reduce the heat and
   simmer for 5 minutes.

2. Take a little of the liquid out of the saucepan and add
   it to a cup with the cornflour. Mix well until the cornflour
   has dissolved, then stir this mixture into the sauce.

3. Cook for a further 1–2 minutes until the sauce has
   thickened.

4. Transfer to a blender and blitz until smooth.

5. The sauce will keep in a sealed jar in the fridge
   for up to 1 week.

INDEX

apple sauce 186
  chocolate chip peanut butter muffins 136
  Finn's sweet potato chocolate cake 164
  healthier pop tarts 42
apples
  apple and carrot chicken balls 91
  apple sauce 186
  chicken and aubergine katsu 94
  fruit salad popsicles 143
  fruity veggie curry 89
  healthier pop tarts 42
asparagus, toad in the hole 103
aubergine, chicken and aubergine katsu 94

bacon
  batch-cook bolognese 79
  toastie pitta pockets 54
  vegetable cornbread 147
baking powder
  banana and blueberry loaves 30
  carrot and orange Greek yoghurt
    muffins 135
  chocolate chip peanut butter muffins 136
  Finn's sweet potato chocolate cake 164
  oaty chocolate biscuits 134
  peanut butter brownies 161
  strawberry banana bread 33
  vegetable cornbread 147
bananas
  banana and blueberry loaves 30
  banana milk 168
  caramelised banana breakfast parfait 45
  chocolate banana overnight oats 28
  chocolate chip peanut butter muffins 136
  chocolate orange nice-cream 144
  fruit and nut breakfast cookies 27
  fruity pancakes 41
  healthier pop tarts 42
  mint choc chip nice-cream 145
  peanut butter nice-cream 144
  quinoa smoothie 171
  raspberry ripple nice cream 145
  strawberry banana bread 33
  strawberry quinoa breakfast bars 24
basil
  hidden veggie tomato sauce 82
  Popeye's protein pesto 78
  strawberry and basil water 167
beef
  batch-cook bolognese 79
  beef and pearl barley casserole 99
  melty mozzarella beef burger 115
  smoky meatball pasta bake 81
beef stock
  batch-cook bolognese 79
  beef and pearl barley casserole 99
  smoky meatball pasta bake 81
black beans, peanut butter brownies 161
blueberries
  banana and blueberry loaves 30
  blueberry and mint water 167
  fruit salad popsicles 143

tutti frutti frozen yoghurt bark 141
bolognese, batch-cook 79
breadcrumbs
  cheese and chive rolls 61
  chicken and aubergine katsu 94
  lentil veggie burger 111
  tuna meatballs 105
broccoli
  broccoli and cheese quesadilla 53
  lentil veggie burger 111
  toad in the hole 103
  tortilla quiche 50
  vegetable cornbread 147
burgers
  lentil veggie burger 111
  melty mozzarella beef burger 115
  tropical chicken burger 112
butter
  Aoife's carrot cake 165
  banana and blueberry loaves 30
  carrot and orange Greek yoghurt
    muffins 135
  cheesy cheddar crackers 151
  chocolate chip granola bars 131
  corn on the cob 118
  cranberry and coconut 133
  creamy cauliflower mashed potato 121
  Finn's sweet potato chocolate cake 164
  fruity flapjacks 127
  hidden veggie risotto 86
  oaty chocolate biscuits 134
  raspberry chia crumble squares 163
  seeded oatcakes 150
  spinach and cheese muffins 67
  strawberry banana bread 33
  vegetable cornbread 147
  veggie egg scramble 35
butternut squash
  fruity veggie curry 89
  hidden veggie risotto 86
  lentil veggie burger 111

cakes
  Aoife's carrot cake 165
  Finn's sweet potato chocolate cake 164
  peanut butter brownies 161
  raspberry chia crumble squares 163
cannellini beans on toast 39
carrots
  Aoife's carrot cake 165
  apple and carrot chicken balls 91
  batch-cook bolognese 79
  carrot and orange Greek yoghurt
    muffins 135
  carrot and orange smoothie 170
  fruity veggie curry 89
  hidden veggie risotto 86
  hidden veggie sausage rolls 62
  hidden veggie tomato sauce 82
  lentil veggie burger 111
  salad cups 117
  sesame chicken noodles 76

seven veg lentil lasagne 83
tortilla quiche 50
tuna meatballs 105
vegetable cornbread 147
casserole, beef and pearl barley 99
cauliflower
  cauliflower cheese cakes 66
  creamy cauliflower mashed potato 121
  hidden veggie risotto 86
  lentil veggie burger 111
celery
  batch-cook bolognese 79
  hidden veggie tomato sauce 82
  seven veg lentil lasagne 83
  tomato and lentil soup with Parmesan
    crisps 56
cheese 69, 70
  cheese and tomato baked risotto 87
  cheesy chicken fritters lunchbox 70
  toastie pitta pockets 54
cheese, Cheddar
  breakfast frittata 38
  broccoli and cheese quesadilla 53
  cauliflower cheese cakes 66
  cheese and chive rolls 61
  cheese and tomato baked risotto 87
  cheesy cheddar crackers 151
  cheesy chicken fritters 59
  chicken and veggie frittata fingers 49
  egg and spinach breakfast pocket 36
  lentil veggie burger 111
  seven veg lentil lasagne 83
  smoky meatball pasta bake 81
  spinach and cheese muffins 67
  tortilla quiche 50
  vegetable cornbread 147
  veggie egg scramble 35
  veggie pizza roll-ups 65
cheese, mozzarella, smoky meatball pasta
  bake 81
cheese, Parmesan
  cauliflower cheese cakes 66
  cheese and chive rolls 61
  cheesy cheddar crackers 151
  creamy roasted pepper pasta sauce 75
  hidden veggie tomato sauce 82
  pesto salmon bake with couscous 106
  Popeye's protein pesto 78
  seven veg lentil lasagne 83
  tomato and lentil soup with Parmesan
    crisps 56
chia seeds
  fruit and nut breakfast cookies 27
  raspberry chia jam 179
chicken
  apple and carrot chicken balls 91
  cheesy chicken fritters 59
  chicken and aubergine katsu 94
  chicken, chorizo and prawn paella 84
  chicken dippers with honey mustard
    mayo 98
  chicken and veggie frittata fingers 49

Greek chicken traybake 97
  piri piri spatchcock chicken 92
  sesame chicken noodles 76
  sweet and sour chicken 95
  tropical chicken burger 112
  tuna bites 55
chickpeas, fruity veggie curry 89
chives
  cheese and chive rolls 61
  cheese and tomato baked risotto 87
chocolate
  chocolate banana overnight oats 28
  chocolate chip energy bites 128
  chocolate chip granola bars 131
  chocolate chip peanut butter muffins 13
  chocolate granola 23
  chocolate nut frozen yoghurt bark 141
  chocolate orange energy bites 130
  chocolate orange tart 158
  Finn's sweet potato chocolate cake 164
  mint choc chip nice-cream 145
  oaty chocolate biscuits 134
  strawberry and chocolate popsicles 143
chocolate-hazelnut spread 183
  chocolate milk 168
  healthier pop tarts 42
chorizo, chicken, chorizo and prawn
  paella 84
cinnamon
  Aoife's carrot cake 165
  banana and blueberry loaves 30
  caramelised banana breakfast parfait 45
  fruity pancakes 41
  gingerbread hot chocolate 174
  healthier pop tarts 42
  raspberry chia crumble squares 163
clementines
  Aoife's carrot cake 165
  fruity flapjacks 127
  rhubarb and strawberry custard
    pots 160
cocoa powder
  chocolate banana overnight oats 28
  chocolate granola 23
  chocolate milk 168
  chocolate orange nice cream 144
  chocolate orange tart 158
  chocolate-hazelnut spread 183
  Finn's sweet potato chocolate cake 164
  gingerbread hot chocolate 174
  peanut butter brownies 161
coconut, desiccated
  chocolate chip energy bites 128
  chocolate orange energy bites 130
  cranberry and coconut 133
  fruity flapjacks 127
  mango and coconut popsicles 142
  mango, lime and coconut energy
    bites 128
  no-sugar rice pudding 157
  raspberry coconut energy bites 130
coconut flakes, healthier pop tarts 42

coconut milk
  chocolate orange tart 158
  mango and coconut popsicles 142
  no-sugar rice pudding 157
  one-pot salmon linguine 109
coconut water, green smoothie 171
cookies
  cranberry and coconut 133
  oaty chocolate biscuits 134
corn
  on the cob 118
  tortilla quiche 50
cornbread, vegetable 147
cornflour
  chilli sauce 187
  crispy sweet potato fries 120
  raspberry chia crumble squares 163
  rhubarb and strawberry custard pots 160
  sesame chicken noodles 76
  sweet and sour chicken 95
courgettes
  fruity veggie curry 89
  hidden veggie sausage rolls 62
  hidden veggie tomato sauce 82
  rainbow veggie kebabs 123
  seven veg lentil lasagne 83
  vegetable cornbread 147
couscous, pesto salmon bake with 106
cranberry and coconut cookies 133
cream
  gingerbread hot chocolate 174
  healthier Eton mess 157
cream cheese
  Aoife's carrot cake 165
  broccoli and cheese quesadilla 53
  cheesy chicken fritters 59
  creamy roasted pepper pasta sauce 75
crème fraîche
  cauliflower cheese cakes 66
  cheesy chicken fritters 59
  chicken and veggie frittata fingers 49
  seven veg lentil lasagne 83
cucumber
  Greek chicken traybake 97
  lentil veggie burger 111
  lime and cucumber water 167
  melty mozzarella beef burger 115
  tropical chicken burger 112
cumin, chicken dippers with honey
  mustard mayo 98
curry
  chicken and aubergine katsu 94
  fruity veggie curry 89
curry powder
  chicken and aubergine katsu 94
  one-pot salmon linguine 109

dates, chocolate orange tart 158
desserts
  chocolate orange tart 158
  healthier Eton mess 157
  no-sugar pudding 157
  rhubarb and strawberry custard
    pots 160
dried fruit
  chocolate granola 23
  fruit and nut breakfast cookies 27
  fruity flapjacks 127
  fruity veggie curry 89

eggs
  Aoife's carrot cake 165
  banana and blueberry loaves 30
  breakfast frittata 38
  carrot and orange Greek yoghurt
    muffins 135
  cauliflower cheese cakes 66
  cheese and chive rolls 61
  cheesy chicken fritters 59
  chicken and aubergine katsu 94
  chicken dippers with honey mustard
    mayo 98
  chicken and veggie frittata fingers 49
  chocolate chip peanut butter muffins 136
  easy mayonnaise 185
  egg and spinach breakfast pocket 36
  fruity pancakes 41
  healthier pop tarts 42
  lentil veggie burger 111
  melty mozzarella beef burger 115
  peanut butter brownies 161
  porridge bread 29
  rhubarb and strawberry custard pots 160
  smoky meatball pasta bake 81
  spinach and cheese muffins 67
  strawberry banana bread 33
  toad in the hole 103
  tortilla quiche 50
  tropical chicken burger 112
  tuna bites 55
  tuna meatballs 105
  vegetable cornbread 147
  veggie egg scramble 35
  veggie pizza roll-ups 65
energy bites
  chocolate chip 128
  chocolate orange 130
  mango, lime and coconut 128
  raspberry coconut 130

fish
  chicken, chorizo, prawn paella 84
  one-pot salmon linguine 109
  pesto salmon bake with couscous 106
  tuna bites 55
  tuna, mayo and corn toastie pitta
    pockets 54
  tuna meatballs 105
flavoured milk
  banana 168
  chocolate 168
  strawberry 168
flavoured water
  blueberry and mint 167
  lime and cucumber 167
  orange and kiwi 167
  strawberry and basil 167
flaxseed
  chocolate chip energy bites 128
  chocolate chip peanut butter muffins 136
  chocolate orange energy bites 130
  mango, lime and coconut energy
    bites 128
  raspberry coconut energy bites 130
food philosophy 8
frittata, breakfast 38
fruit 8
fussy eating
  break the routine 13

  get children involved 12
  hidden veggies 13
  make it fun 12–13
  one step at a time 12
  positive language 12
  relax 10
  sensory issues 13
  slow introduction of new food 11
  understanding 11

garlic cloves
  beans on toast 39
  breakfast frittata 38
  cauliflower cheese cakes 66
  cheese and tomato baked risotto 87
  chicken and aubergine katsu 94
  chicken, chorizo and prawn paella 84
  chilli sauce 187
  corn on the cob 118
  creamy roasted pepper pasta sauce 75
  fruity veggie curry 89
  Greek chicken traybake 97
  hidden veggie sausage rolls 62
  hidden veggie tomato sauce 82
  lentil veggie burger 111
  melty mozzarella beef burger 115
  one-pot salmon linguine 109
  Popeye's protein pesto 78
  sesame chicken noodles 76
  smoky meatball pasta bake 80–1
  sweet and sour chicken 95
  tomato and lentil soup with Parmesan
    crisps 56
  tropical chicken burger 112
  tuna bites 55
  tuna meatballs 105
garlic powder, sweet potato hash
    browns 35
ginger, gingerbread hot chocolate 174
granola
  caramelised banana breakfast parfait 45
  yoghurt pudding pops 139

ham
  ham and cheese wrap lunchbox 70
  toastie pitta pockets 54
  tortilla quiche 50
  tuna bites 55
hazelnuts, chocolate-hazelnut spread 183
herbs, dried
  apple and carrot chicken balls 91
  beans on toast 39
  chicken, chorizo and prawn paella 84
  crispy sweet potato fries 120
  garlic and herb breadsticks 153
  Greek chicken traybake 97
  lentil veggie burger 111
  melty mozzarella beef burger 115
  rainbow veggie kebabs 123
  tuna meatballs 105
herbs, fresh, seven veg lentil lasagne 83
herbs, Italian
  batch-cook bolognese 79
  crispy sweet potato fries 120
  easy potato wedges 120
  garlic and herb breadsticks 153
  hidden veggie tomato sauce 82
  lentil veggie burger 111
  smoky meatball pasta bake 81

hidden veggies 13
  risotto 86
  sausage rolls 62
  tomato sauce 82
honey
  Aoife's carrot cake 165
  banana and blueberry loaves 30
  beans on toast 39
  caramelised banana breakfast parfait 45
  carrot and orange Greek yoghurt
    muffins 135
  chicken dippers with honey mustard mayo 98
  chilli sauce 187
  chocolate banana overnight oats 28
  chocolate chip energy bites 128
  chocolate chip granola bars 131
  chocolate chip peanut butter muffins 136
  chocolate milk 168
  chocolate nut frozen yoghurt bark 141
  chocolate orange energy bites 130
  chocolate orange nice cream 144
  chocolate-hazelnut spread 183
  fruit and nut breakfast cookies 27
  fruity flapjacks 127
  gingerbread hot chocolate 174
  Greek chicken traybake 97
  healthier Eton mess 157
  healthy strawberry lemonade 170
  kiddie ketchup 185
  mango and coconut popsicles 142
  mango, lime and coconut energy bites 128
  oaty chocolate biscuits 134
  peanut butter 180
  peanut butter brownies 161
  piri piri spatchcock chicken 92
  quinoa smoothie 171
  raspberry chia crumble squares 163
  raspberry chia jam 179
  raspberry coconut energy bites 130
  rhubarb and strawberry custard
    pots 160
  sesame chicken noodles 76
  strawberry banana bread 33
  strawberry and chocolate popsicles 143
  sunflower butter 180
  sweet and sour chicken 95
  tutti frutti frozen yoghurt bark 141
hot chocolate, gingerbread 174
hummus 70

ice-cream
  chocolate orange nice cream 144
  mint choc chip nice-cream 145
  peanut butter nice cream 144
  raspberry ripple nice-cream 145

kebabs, rainbow veggie 123
ketchup, kiddie 185
kitchen gadgets
  colourful plates, bowls, cutlery 15
  electric scales 15
  electric whisk 15
  food processor 15
  garlic crusher 15
  hand-held blender 15
  ice cream scoop 15
  lunchboxes 15
  silicone baking sheet 15
  stand blender 15

kiwis
  fruit salad popsicles 143
  orange and kiwi water 167
  tutti frutti frozen yoghurt bark 141

lemons
  chicken, chorizo and prawn paella 84
  easy mayonnaise 185
  Greek chicken traybake 97
  healthy strawberry lemonade 170
  Popeye's protein pesto 78
  tuna meatballs 105
lettuce
  apple and carrot chicken balls 91
  cheesy chicken fritters 59
  lentil veggie burger 111
  melty mozzarella beef burger 115
  salad cups 117
  toastie pitta pockets 54
  tropical chicken burger 112
limes
  fruity party slushes 173
  lime and cucumber water 167
  mango, lime and coconut energy
    bites 128
  tropical chicken burger 112

mango chutney, fruity veggie curry 89
mangos
  green smoothie 171
  mango and coconut popsicles 142
  mango, lime and coconut energy
    bites 128
  tropical chicken burger 112
maple syrup
  chocolate banana overnight oats 28
  fruit and nut breakfast cookies 27
mayonnaise
  chicken dippers with honey mustard
    mayo 98
  easy mayonnaise 185
  toastie pitta pockets 54
meal plans 12
  less food waste 17
  less stress 17
  saving money 17
  saving time 17
  suggestions for four weeks 18–19
meringue, healthier Eton mess 157
milk
  chocolate banana overnight oats 28
  chocolate chip peanut butter muffins 136
  chocolate-hazelnut spread 183
  creamy cauliflower mashed potato 121
  fruity pancakes 41
  gingerbread hot chocolate 174
  hidden veggie risotto 86
  peanut butter brownies 161
  porridge bread 29
  quinoa smoothie 171
  rhubarb and strawberry custard pots 160
  spinach and cheese muffins 67
  strawberry shortcake overnight oats 28
  toad in the hole 103
  vegetable cornbread 147
  see also flavoured milk
mint leaves
  blueberry and mint water 167
  mint choc chip nice-cream 145

mint sauce, Greek chicken traybake 97
mixed berries
  fruity flapjacks 127
  fruity pancakes 41
  quinoa smoothie 171
mixed nuts
  chocolate granola 23
  chocolate orange tart 158
  fruit and nut breakfast cookies 27
mixed seeds
  chocolate granola 23
  fruit and nut breakfast cookies 27
  fruity flapjacks 127
  porridge bread 29
  seeded oatcakes 150
mixed vegetables
  chicken and veggie frittata fingers 49
  pesto salmon bake with couscous 106
  savoury veggie rice 117
  tortilla quiche 50
  tuna bites 55
  veggie pizza roll-ups 65
muffins
  carrot and orange Greek yoghurt
    muffins 135
  chocolate chip peanut butter muffins 136
mushrooms
  beef and pearl barley casserole 99
  rainbow veggie kebabs 123
mustard, Dijon
  breakfast frittata 38
  cheese and chive rolls 61
  chicken dippers with honey mustard
    mayo 98
  kiddie ketchup 185
  toad in the hole 103
mustard, English, easy mayonnaise 185
mustard, wholegrain, cauliflower cheese
  cakes 66

nutmeg, gingerbread hot chocolate 174

olives, Greek chicken traybake 97
onions
  apple and carrot chicken balls 91
  batch-cook bolognese 79
  beef and pearl barley casserole 99
  cheese and tomato baked risotto 87
  chicken and aubergine katsu 94
  chicken, chorizo and prawn paella 84
  fruity veggie curry 89
  Greek chicken traybake 97
  hidden veggie tomato sauce 82
  lentil veggie burger 111
  rainbow veggie kebabs 123
  seven veg lentil lasagne 83
  sweet and sour chicken 95
  tomato and lentil soup with Parmesan
    crisps 56
orange juice
  carrot and orange smoothie 170
  chocolate orange energy bites 130
  chocolate orange nice cream 144
  fruit and nut breakfast cookies 27
  fruity flapjacks 127
oranges
  carrot and orange Greek yoghurt
    muffins 135
  chocolate orange tart 158

fruit and nut breakfast cookies 27
  orange and kiwi water 167
oregano
  creamy roasted pepper pasta sauce 75
  Greek chicken traybake 97
  melty mozzarella beef burger 115
  seven veg lentil lasagne 83
  tuna meatballs 105
  veggie pizza roll-ups 65

paella, chicken, chorizo, prawn 84
passata
  beans on toast 39
  hidden veggie tomato sauce 82
  kiddie ketchup 185
  smoky meatball pasta bake 80–1
pasta
  creamy roasted pepper pasta sauce 75
  one-pot salmon linguine 109
  sesame chicken noodles 76
  seven veg lentil lasagne 83
  smoky meatball pasta bake 81
  tuna meatballs 105
pastry, puff
  cheese and chive rolls 61
  hidden veggie sausage rolls 62
  sweet and savoury pastry straws 148
  veggie pizza roll-ups 65
pastry, shortcrust, healthier pop tarts 42
peaches
  fruit salad popsicles 143
  tutti frutti frozen yoghurt bark 141
peanut butter 180
  chocolate chip energy bites 128
  chocolate chip granola bars 131
  chocolate chip peanut butter muffins 136
  chocolate orange energy bites 130
  healthier pop tarts 42
  mango, lime and coconut energy
    bites 128
  nice-cream 144
  peanut butter brownies 161
  raspberry coconut energy bites 130
peanuts
  chocolate nut frozen yoghurt bark 141
  peanut butter 180
pearl barley, beef and pearl barley
  casserole 99
peas
  chicken, chorizo and prawn paella 84
  fruity veggie curry 89
  Popeye's protein pesto 78
  sesame chicken noodles 76
  seven veg lentil lasagne 83
  tortilla quiche 50
peppers, green
  pesto salmon bake with couscous 106
  rainbow veggie kebabs 123
peppers, mixed, Greek chicken traybake 97
peppers, red
  broccoli and cheese quesadilla 53
  chicken, chorizo and prawn paella 84
  chilli sauce 187
  creamy roasted pepper pasta sauce 75
  hidden veggie tomato sauce 82
  one-pot salmon linguine 109
  rainbow veggie kebabs 123
  savoury veggie rice 117
  sesame chicken noodles 76

seven veg lentil lasagne 83
  spinach and cheese muffins 67
  tomato and lentil soup with Parmesan
    crisps 56
  tropical chicken burger 112
  vegetable cornbread 147
peppers, sweet, sweet and sour chicken
peppers, yellow
  pesto salmon bake with couscous 106
  salad cups 117
  veggie egg scramble 35
pesto
  Popeye's protein pesto 78
  sweet and savoury pastry straws 148
pineapple
  fruity party slushes 173
  green smoothie 171
  sweet and sour chicken 95
  tropical chicken burger 112
piri piri spatchcock chicken 92
pitta bread, toastie pitta pockets 54
polenta, vegetable cornbread 147
pop tarts, healthier 42
popcorn 70
poppy seeds
  cheese and chive rolls 61
  hidden veggie sausage rolls 62
popsicles
  fruit salad 143
  mango and coconut 142
  strawberry and chocolate 143
  watermelon and kiwi 142
porridge bread 29
portion sizes 14
potatoes
  cauliflower cheese cakes 66
  creamy cauliflower mashed potato 121
  easy potato wedges 120
  lentil veggie burger 111
  sweet potato hash browns 35
prawns
  chicken, chorizo and prawn paella 84
  tuna bites 55
puffed rice cereal, chocolate chip granola
  bars 131
pumpkin seeds, Popeye's protein pesto 78

quinoa
  apple and carrot chicken balls 91
  smoothie 171
  strawberry quinoa breakfast bars 24

raisins
  Aoife's carrot cake 165
  fruity veggie curry 89
  strawberry quinoa breakfast bars 24
raspberries
  no-sugar pudding 157
  raspberry chia jam 179
  raspberry coconut energy bites 130
  raspberry ripple nice-cream 145
  tutti frutti frozen yoghurt bark 141
raspberry chia jam 179
  healthier pop tarts 42
  raspberry chia crumble squares 163
  sweet and savoury pastry straws 148
red chilli, chilli sauce 187
red lentils
  seven veg lentil lasagne 83

tomato and lentil soup with Parmesan
   crisps 56
ed wine 14
   batch-cook bolognese 79
   beef and pearl barley casserole 99
   smoky meatball pasta bake 81
   hubarb and strawberry custard pots 160
ce
   cheese and tomato baked risotto 87
   chicken and aubergine katsu 94
   chicken, chorizo and prawn paella 84
   fruity veggie curry 89
   hidden veggie risotto 86
   no-sugar rice pudding 157
   savoury veggie rice 117
   tuna bites 55
ce cakes 69
ice wine vinegar, sweet and sour
   chicken 95
olled oats
   chocolate banana overnight oats 28
   chocolate chip energy bites 128
   chocolate chip granola bars 131
   chocolate chip peanut butter muffins 136
   chocolate granola 23
   chocolate orange energy bites 130
   cranberry and coconut 133
   fruity flapjacks 127
   fruity pancakes 41
   oaty chocolate biscuits 134
   porridge bread 29
   raspberry chia crumble squares 163
   seeded oatcakes 150
   strawberry quinoa breakfast bars 24
   strawberry shortcake overnight oats 28
osemary
   chicken, chorizo and prawn paella 84
   seven veg lentil lasagne 83

saffron, chicken, chorizo and prawn
   paella 84
sage, apple and carrot chicken balls 91
salad cups 117
sauces
   chilli sauce 187
   creamy roasted pepper pasta sauce 75
   hidden veggie tomato sauce 82
   kiddie ketchup 185
   sweet chilli 187
sausage meat
   breakfast frittata 38
   hidden veggie sausage rolls 62
sausages
   sausage roll lunchbox 69
   sausage skewers lunchbox 70
   toad in the hole 103
sesame seeds
   cheese and chive rolls 61
   hidden veggie sausage rolls 62
   Popeye's protein pesto 78
   sesame chicken noodles 76
shallots
   beans on toast 39
   melty mozzarella beef burger 115
   one-pot salmon linguine 109
   smoky meatball pasta bake 81
slushies, fruity party 173
smoked paprika
   beans on toast 39

cheesy cheddar crackers 151
chicken, chorizo and prawn paella 84
crispy sweet potato fries 120
Greek chicken traybake 97
hidden veggie tomato sauce 82
lentil veggie burger 111
piri piri spatchcock chicken 92
seven veg lentil lasagne 83
smoky meatball pasta bake 80–1
tomato and lentil soup with Parmesan
   crisps 56
smoothies
   carrot and orange 170
   green 171
   leftover smoothie pops 139
   quinoa 171
soup, tomato and lentil with Parmesan
   crisps 56
sourdough bread, beans on toast 39
soy sauce
   chicken and aubergine katsu 94
   sesame chicken noodles 76
   sweet and sour chicken 95
   tuna bites 55
spinach
   cheese and chive rolls 61
   egg and spinach breakfast pocket 36
   fruity veggie curry 89
   green smoothie 171
   mint choc chip nice-cream 145
   Popeye's protein pesto 78
   seven veg lentil lasagne 83
   spinach and cheese muffin lunchbox 69
   spinach and cheese muffins 67
   tropical chicken burger 112
   vegetable cornbread 147
   veggie egg scramble 35
spring onions
   breakfast frittata 38
   cauliflower cheese cakes 66
   sesame chicken noodles 76
   spinach and cheese muffins 67
   tropical chicken burger 112
   tuna bites 55
   tuna meatballs 105
   vegetable cornbread 147
store cupboard essentials
   dairy, meat, eggs 16
   dried goods 16
   frozen goods 16
   fruit and vegetables (fresh and frozen) 16
   herbs and spices 16
   tins, jars, cartons, bottles 16
strawberries
   fruit salad popsicles 143
   healthier Eton mess 157
   healthy strawberry lemonade 170
   no-sugar rice pudding 157
   rhubarb and strawberry custard pots 160
   strawberry banana bread 33
   strawberry and basil water 167
   strawberry and chocolate popsicles 143
   strawberry milk 168
   strawberry quinoa breakfast bars 24
   strawberry shortcake overnight oats 28
   tutti frutti frozen yoghurt bark 141
   yoghurt pudding pops 139
strawberry jam, strawberry shortcake
   overnight oats 28

sugar 9
   cranberry and coconut 133
   Finn's sweet potato chocolate cake 164
   raspberry chia crumble squares 163
sunflower seeds
   Popeye's protein pesto 78
   sunflower butter 180
sweet potatoes
   crispy sweet potato fries 120
   Finn's sweet potato chocolate cake 164
   hidden veggie risotto 86
   sweet potato hash browns 35
sweetcorn
   broccoli and cheese quesadilla 53
   one-pot salmon linguine 109
   sesame chicken noodles 76
   seven veg lentil lasagne 83
   toastie pitta pockets 54
   tropical chicken burger 112

thyme, seven veg lentil lasagne 83
tomato purée
   batch-cook bolognese 79
   beans on toast 39
   beef and pearl barley casserole 99
   fruity veggie curry 89
   hidden veggie tomato sauce 82
   kiddie ketchup 185
   seven veg lentil lasagne 83
   sweet and sour chicken 95
   tomato and lentil soup with Parmesan
     crisps 56
   tuna meatballs 105
   veggie pizza roll-ups 65
tomatoes
   batch-cook bolognese 79
   cheese and tomato baked risotto 87
   creamy roasted pepper pasta sauce 75
   lentil veggie burger 111
   melty mozzarella beef burger 115
   pesto salmon bake with couscous 106
   toastie pitta pockets 54
   tomato and lentil soup with Parmesan
     crisps 56
   tropical chicken burger 112
   tuna meatballs 105
tomatoes, cherry
   breakfast frittata 38
   cheese and tomato baked risotto 87
   Greek chicken traybake 97
   pesto salmon bake with couscous 106
   rainbow veggie kebabs 123
   salad cups 117
   tortilla quiche 50
   veggie egg scramble 35
tortilla wraps
   broccoli and cheese quesadilla 53
   egg and spinach breakfast pocket 36
   salad cups 117
   tortilla quiche 50
turkey salad wrap lunchbox 70
turmeric
   chicken, chorizo and prawn paella 84
   savoury veggie rice 117

vegetable stock
   cauliflower cheese cakes 66
   cheese and tomato baked risotto 87
   chicken and aubergine katsu 94

hidden veggie risotto 86
hidden veggie tomato sauce 82
pesto salmon bake with couscous 106
savoury veggie rice 117
seven veg lentil lasagne 83
spinach and cheese muffins 67
tomato and lentil soup with Parmesan
   crisps 56
vegetables 8

walnuts, Aoife's carrot cake 165
water 8
watermelon, fruity party slushes 173
white wine vinegar, chilli sauce 187
Worcestershire sauce
   beans on toast 39
   smoky meatball pasta bake 81

yeast, garlic and herb breadsticks 153
yoghurt
   banana and blueberry loaves 30
   carrot and orange smoothie 170
   chocolate banana overnight oats 28
   porridge bread 29
   quinoa smoothie 171
   sausage roll lunchbox 69
   strawberry and chocolate popsicles 143
   strawberry shortcake overnight oats 28
yoghurt, frozen
   chocolate nut 141
   tutti frutti 141
   yoghurt pudding pops 139
yoghurt, Greek
   caramelised banana breakfast parfait 45
   carrot and orange Greek yoghurt
     muffins 135
   Finn's sweet potato chocolate cake 164
   Greek chicken traybake 97
   healthier Eton mess 157

ACKNOWLEDGEMENTS

Without a doubt, my first thank you has to go to all my blog readers and social media followers.
Your comments, likes and shares have allowed me to turn my passion into a job that I absolutely love
and I will for ever be grateful for your kindness and support.
To my wonderful agent Sarah, thank you for believing in this book before it even existed
and for your encouragement every step of the way.
To Natalie at Bonnier, thank you for giving me the opportunity to turn this book from a dream into reality.
And to Lizzie and September, thank you for all your hard work behind the scenes.
To Kim, Becci and Catherine, thank you for bringing the recipes to life with your beautiful photography and food
and prop styling. And to Morwenna, my first editor, and Elizabeth, my current editor, Mark and the design team,
and illustrator Lucy, thank you for turning this simple collection of recipes into a vibrant and colourful book
that I couldn't be more proud to put my name to.
To my Headcorn friends, thank you for allowing me to use your children as taste-testers, for your help with childcare
and for taking me in for wine and chats on the days when things weren't going so well.
To my husband for your love and encouragement from day one, thank you. You've had more belief in me than
I've had in myself these last few years and I will always be so thankful for that.
To my mother and mother-in-law, I am very lucky to have two very supportive and strong female role models in my life.
You have both encouraged me to follow my dreams and your hard work over the years will always be appreciated.
And finally, to the two lights of my life, Aoife and Fintan. Aoife, you made me a mum and changed my world for ever.
You inspired me to start this whole project more than four years ago and you continue to inspire me every day
with your eternal happiness and optimism. Fintan, you are one in a million, the most special little
boy a mother could ever wish for and you make me proud every single day.